DATE DUE			

Love and Marriage in Chrétien de Troyes

PETER S. NOBLE

CARDIFF
UNIVERSITY OF WALES PRESS
1982

British Library Cataloguing in Publication Data
Noble, Peter S.
   Love and marriage in Chrétien de Troyes.
   1. Chrétien, *de Troyes*—Criticism and interpretation
   2. Love in Literature
   I. Title
   841'.1   PQ1450.L6

ISBN 0-7083-0805-8
ISBN 0-7083-0835X

Printed by The Cambrian News (Aberystwyth) Ltd.

TO
MY PARENTS

CONTENTS

PREFACE

My aim in this book is to demonstrate the originality of Chrétien de Troyes as shown by his treatment of the theme of love. That this theme is only one of many in Chrétien's work is obvious, but it is one which clearly interested him and which tells us much about the period in which he was writing. His influence on European literature is undeniable, and his ability to fascinate those who read him to-day is due in part to his treatment of love, as we can recognise behind the glamour of the Arthurian setting people trying to understand and live with emotions and problems which are as real to-day as they were in the twelfth century. I hope to convey something of the skill and insight of Chrétien and perhaps to encourage more people to read him for themselves.

It is a pleasure to thank all those who have helped to make this book possible. I am grateful to the Board of the University of Wales Press who accepted it.. The late Dr L. T. Topsfield introduced me to the works of Chrétien and inspired my interest in them. It is a particular sorrow that he did not live to see this book which owes so much to him and that his own book on Chrétien appeared after this one was in the hands of the publishers. I owe a special debt to Professor W. G. van Emden who read the first draft and to Professors D. J. A. Ross and A. Diverres who read the completed version. Their suggestions were most helpful but they are in no way responsible for the shortcomings of my work. Mrs Erika Stockbridge typed the book for me and I am most grateful for her kindness. Finally I must pay tribute to my wife without whose devoted help, patience and advice this book would certainly never have been written.

INTRODUCTION

Whatever attitude one takes to the development of emotional relationships between men and women, it is clear that in the late eleventh and twelfth centuries there was a considerable and growing interest in the feelings which men and women had for each other and in the way in which they expressed them. The vernacular literatures in France, both in the Langue d'oc and the Langue d'oil, bear witness to this interest, since love becomes an increasingly important topic, even invading a genre such as epic in which it had originally a relatively small role to play. The *Chanson de Roland* shows little interest in the love, if any, between Roland and Aude, who enters the poem only to die immediately of a broken heart. The poet is instead more concerned with the companionship of Roland and Oliver, which is very much part of the masculine, military society which he is depicting.

That there was an audience for something different before 1100, in the south of France at least, is demonstrated by the appearance of the poems of Guillaume ix, which are the first surviving vernacular poems treating of love in a variety of forms. Thereafter the nature of love is examined by more and more poets bearing witness to the growth in interest in love and in analysing it. That there are likely to be differences in their approaches and their interests would seem self-evident, but it has been ignored by some critics who have tended to classify such poets as writing in the tradition of *amour courtois* and *courtoisie,* which a few critics have failed to distinguish.[1] There should be little excuse for such a failing after the work of critics such as Moshé Lazar,[2] but there is still a lively controversy as to how to describe the love described by twelfth-century authors. *Amour courtois* is still much used, as a general, cover-all term, although F. L. Utley favours replacing it with *fine amour,* which seems to him a more precise term and less likely to cause confusion.[3] Still other critics, such as D. W. Robertson, jnr., or John Moore, reject the whole idea of courtly love or *amour courtois.* 'Let us avoid the term *courtly love.* It was rarely used before Gaston Paris, and it has preserved the mistaken notion that there was one, clearly defined kind of love celebrated in the courts. The "true" or "pure" or "fine" love of which the poets sang, was, in the phrase of Maurice Valency, "a spectrum of attitudes".[4] Robertson is even more dismissive. 'The study of courtly love, if it belongs anywhere, should be conducted only as this subject is an aspect of nineteenth and twentieth century cultural history.'[5] This argument was severely criticised by Frappier with considerable justice.[6]

There is an argument to be made which suggests that courtly love (I intend to use the English form) implies a nineteenth-century interpretation of a twelfth-century phenomenon. The whole concept of the faithful knight, serving his lady with selfless devotion, hardly daring to hope for a reward can be shown to be relatively rare in medieval romance.[7] On the other hand it is convenient to have a term to describe the tremendous interest in love which undoubtedly existed in the twelfth century, provided it is also realised that each author is an individual and may well add something of his own to his treatment of love.[8] The term *fine amour* has much to recommend it, although it runs the risk of being confused with *fin 'amors* which, as Lazar has shown, is not at all the same thing. 'Mais en passant du Midi dans le Nord, l'idéologie de l'amour courtois s'est transformée. Elle a abandonné en cours de route une partie de sa densité érotique, et surtout, son exaltation de l'adultère (les romans de *Tristan* et de *Lancelot* exceptés). L'amour a pris un aspect plus réaliste.'[9] This conclusion cannot, however, be applied to all northern authors as Bartina Wind makes clear. 'L'auteur fait sans doute allusion ici à Chrétien de Troyes et à Marie de France, mais ces auteurs ne sont plus exclusivement et typiquement courtois.'[10]

Different terms are therefore necessary to describe northern and southern ideas on love, because the differences between the two sets of ideas are too great to be covered by one common term. *Fin'amors* does seem to be the term generally accepted to describe the southern concept, but *amour courtois* or courtly love for the north is challenged not only on the grounds of inaccuracy but also because its very existence as a concept has been questioned. Even amongst those who accept the term courtly love as one which describes a coherent set of ideas on love and the behaviour of lovers there are disputes, as Wind indicates, over which authors should be considered as writing within the code of courtly love. Here too there is need for care as a courtly writer may not be writing about courtly love, a point which Wind does not make clear. After all a writer could still merit the epithet courtly, if he were writing about courts and the behaviour associated with them, even if he were not mainly concerned with love in any form. Courtly love will take place within a courtly setting, that is at a court where a refined standard of behaviour and a keen appreciation of emotional subtlety can be expected. I intend to use the terms courtly love and courtliness because they are still probably the most widely used and are therefore convenient. As there is so much controversy about them, however, it seems desirable to examine them further before embarking on an analysis of Chrétien's ideas on love.

The question of origins need not concern us here, especially as it has been so admirably treated by Roger Boase in his recent book[11] which gives an excellent account of the various theories. What is surely clear is that in the late eleventh century a variety of social and intellectual currents were jointly bringing about changes in people's attitudes to many things, not least the relationship between the sexes. One of the most important of these elements was the changing position of women. 'The widening horizons of the eleventh and early twelfth centuries opened new paths; many women rebelled against their enslavement to the marriage bed and their social inferiority, and in an age in which the celibate ideal flourished as never before or since in western Europe they sought escape in ways ascetic as well as carnal.'[12]

Women no longer accepted the secondary role assigned to them in society quite so passively, and this was certain to be reflected in the literature as well. 'Yet it [the twelfth century] was also the age which saw the rise of the romantic tradition, of courtly love and literature. Whatever its origin and background, however much its sentiments may be paralleled in earlier literature in Christendom and Islam, as a fashion generating a vast and flourishing literature it was something new and reflects the inventiveness and variety of fashion and sentiment in the late twelfth and early thirteenth centuries.'[13] Much of the credit for the success of the romantic tradition of this period must be attributed to Chrétien de Troyes whose works are the earliest surviving Arthurian romances and, in the eyes of most critics, reached a standard not to be equalled in verse. Chrétien undoubtedly knew the Provençal tradition. His own surviving lyric poetry contains clear references to Bernart de Ventadorn.[14] He also knew well the Tristan legend against which he reacted with some vigour. 'Cependant le mérite revient à

Chrétien de Troyes d'avoir opposé le plus lucidement à la passion fatale de Tristan et d'Iseut l'essence de l'amour courtois, fondé sur un choix . . .'[15] There must also have been an already existing tradition in the north on which Chrétien could draw.[16]

What seems equally certain is that there was no codified system, no strict set of rules prescribing the appropriate behaviour for the lover at the time when Chrétien was writing. The troubadours of the south were individualists, whose songs cannot be confined within such a restrictive term as amour courtois, '. . . l'expression amour courtois est impropre pour qualifier l'idéologie amoureuse qui s'épanouit au xiie siècle dans une grande diversité d'oeuvres littéraires, et est trop étroite pour pouvoir contenir à la fois l'amour exalté par des troubadours et l'amour proné par un Chrétien de Troyes ou par les trouvères.'[17]

Nevertheless there are certain generalisations which can be made, perhaps the most important being the very secular nature of the love. 'Car la conception d'amour qui surgit dans le Midi, dans les dernières années du xie siècle est une conception nettement opposée à la morale chrétienne . . . indépendante de la société christianisée.'[18] Not only was it secular but it was hostile to marriage: 'Que l'amour courtois ait été antimatrimonial, c'est évident.'[19] and of necessity adulterous: '. . . l'amour courtois est par nature un amour adultère. Il ne saurait en être autrement. L'amour n'existe pas dans le mariage.'[20] Love of this type should be ennobling. 'L'amour courtois reconnaît qu'il a pour origine le désir et l'ultime récompense qu'il souhaite est de pouvoir le satisfaire. Réalistes autant qu'idéalistes, les troubadours estiment donc que céder aux exigences de la chair n'interdit pas d'être élégant. L'essentiel est de s'imposer une attente, et de se plier à une discipline . . . La nécessité d'un effort apparaît ainsi et la conscience des mérites acquis, non sans peine, grâce à cet effort crée une fierté et une espérance exaltante. On peut alors parler de la vertu ennoblissante de l'amour . . .'[21]

Such concepts are clearly in circulation and well known before Chrétien, but they are not more than that. 'A distinction must be made between the established doctrine, a rigid system of rules of behaviour, which did not exist, and a mode of thought, expressed in literary conventions, which can be traced through so much medieval literature. . .'[22] Chrétien had at his disposal the southern tradition of adulterous love for a lady, probably socially superior, who might or might not choose to reward her lover, whose love was in no way platonic but full of sensuality and longing. The lover hoped to earn an improvement in his position by his patient devotion but he was not prepared to be faithful for ever. The love of the troubadours was of necessity self-centred. As they were rarely close to or in contact with the beloved they had to concentrate on their own thoughts and feelings. In addition there was the Tristan legend, already well-known on the continent, with its theme of all-consuming passion imposed by fate, a direct contrast to the reasoned and measured (in theory at least) love of the troubadours. There are also, as already suggested, some independent northern traditions harking back to Geoffrey of Monmouth and Wace. Finally there is the whole mass of Celtic legend apart from Tristan.

There was no code of love, however, and the introduction of Andreas Capellanus seems of dubious value with reference to Chrétien. Andreas almost certainly was writing after Chrétien, and it is highly uncertain whether they even knew each other.[23] The date most favoured for the writing of Andreas' text is 1186,[24] when it seems likely that Andreas was not in the service of the Countess Marie, if he ever had been,[25] and may not have been writing for her.[26] His usefulness in interpreting Chrétien can therefore be easily overestimated. Whatever dates one accepts for the romances of Chrétien, by 1186 his work was, if not complete, at least well advanced. Andreas may be drawing on Chrétien, but Chrétien is certainly not drawing on Andreas. Further as John Stevens has pointed out, the existence of Andreas' book proves very little, '. . . the existence of Andreas Capellanus's treatise, *De Amore,* does not prove the existence of a "code of courtly love". It simply establishes the existence of experiences which could be codified and that there was a fashion for codification.'[27]

Coupled with this is the whole problem of the interpretation of Andreas. Stevens is inclined to dismiss any claim that the writer may have to be taken seriously.[28] For Robertson the work is ironic,[29] but others have taken it at face value, '. . . his . . . is a simple manual for those who wanted to love *honeste,* that is, like gentlemen.'[30] Barbara Nelson Sargent has shown, moreover, that it would be wrong to assume that all medieval readers automatically interpreted the *De Amore* ironically.[31] Father Foster would accept the work as a reliable witness to twelfth-century attitudes.[32]

The scope for argument is limitless, but what Andreas' *De Amore,* whether it is ironical or not, does bear witness to is the intense interest in educated circles in love and more particularly in a sophisticated love which '. . . reflects an enhancement of the position and influence of women in medieval society, in the sphere of sexual relations.'[33] Any links between Andreas and Chrétien de Troyes remain to be proven, and his doctrines cannot be shown to have influenced Chrétien. They do, however, presumably reflect some of the fashionable ideas which were currently in circulation, the chief of which seems to be that love could only be adulterous.[34] This was, of course, in direct conflict with the reality of the period. 'Whether *De Amore* was intended literally or satirically, a point still debated, its ideology, like that of the troubadours is in unmistakable conflict with medieval living realities which stoutly upheld the ancient double standard in respect to adultery.'[35] Reality may well be better depicted in the *chanson de toile* as J-C Payen has suggested,[36] but there love is seen as brutal, a source of pain and tears to the woman, who nearly always has to submit to and justify herself before the man. Nevertheless such poems would also help to arouse public interest in emotional problems and relationships.[37]

Romance, the genre which concentrates above all on love, particularly on the awakening of love, makes little pretence of being realistic. The background of the Arthurian court in some Celtic region, remote in both time and distance from the courts of Champagne and Flanders, gives freedom to writers to meet the wishes and fantasies of their audience, which in the case of women are clearly escapist, seeking a world in which they do exercise authority over men in the sphere of emotions at least. They escape too from the sordid reality of unfaithful husbands, regular child-birth with all its attendant risks and the diseases and dirt of their own, often far from comfortable or glamorous, castles. This unreality becomes clearer and more stressed as the genre continues into the thirteenth century. Chrétien, on the whole, reduces the role of the Celtic *merveilleux* and indeed does not treat it with the seriousness of some of his followers.[38] This means that the Celtic background on which he draws so heavily remains just that, an exotic background, against which his characters can experience recognisable emotions and grapple with recognisable problems. The audience is forced to concentrate on the main character or characters, although there are passages where the emotional tension is relaxed through the use of description or the *merveilleux*.

If we accept that Chrétien was writing for the court of the Countess Marie, as we presumably must, except for *Le Conte du Graal*, then he is writing for a court with a sophisticated audience of high-born women whose many connections with other courts might make them familiar with the material on which he was drawing. They would also know from first hand experience or observation the sort of problems which women had to face. One can surely assume that the life of Eleanor of Aquitaine with its many storms would be familiar to all of them. Her need, after her divorce from Louis of France, to secure a husband quickly to defend her immense possessions would be obvious to all of them, not least because they would remember the attempts to kidnap and abduct her on her way south from Paris. Her problems with Henry's infidelities would also be common knowledge. With examples like this from the lives of people they knew or to whom they were related upper class women would be glad to find release and escape in stories where they were not mere pawns, but could exercise control and influence.

Lyric poetry would already have made them familiar with many of the concepts of love as treated by the troubadours. The *romans d'antiquité* had moved away from the masculine dominated view of life offered by epic and the audience was ready for the next step in the treatment of women and love, which would be taken by the authors of Arthurian romance. Chrétien therefore can be seen to be responding to the interests and the wishes of his time and of the society for which he was writing, but his treatment of love is unexpected given the background against which he was writing and the attitudes expressed by many of his predecessors. As Frappier puts it; 'Chrétien lui aussi est un apologiste du mariage et de l'amour dans le mariage'.[39] That is not enough, however.

Chrétien is not just an apologist for marriage and love in marriage, he is their advocate,[40] constructing three of his romances round this theme and showing the disadvantages of other relationships based, as he sees it, on a less stable foundation. The *Chevalier de la Charrete,* according to Chrétien himself, was not entirely of his own choosing, and he may not have had a wholly free hand in the treatment either, but in it too it is possible to detect an attitude not inconsistent with the attitude of *Erec et Enide, Cligés* and the *Chevalier au Lion. Le Conte du Graal* was written for another patron, Philip of Flanders, a man with very different tastes from those of the Countess Marie, and this must be a factor in explaining the new type of story on which Chrétien had embarked. It may well be that he turned to religion, as he was dissatisfied with the values of earthly love,[41] but love is not absent from *Le Conte du Graal,* and as it is unfinished, we cannot be certain how Chrétien intended to resolve the various problems. Perceval might or might not have returned to marry Blancheflor, but the emphasis on the religious nature of Perceval's quest may well reflect Chrétien's realisation of where the interests of Philip of Flanders lay, while the minor characters and the adventures of Gauvain suggest that Chrétien had by no means lost interest in the problems of love.

Love and its problems are a constant theme in the works of Chrétien de Troyes, but a superficial reading of his work can leave the impression that his attitude changes with each poem. It develops, of course, and he has different things to say in each poem because he is examining different aspects of the relationship between men and women, but, as I have attempted to show elsewhere with regard to the characters who reappear in the romances, Chrétien develops and enriches his interpretation without altering his earlier ideas.[42] So with love he has a clear idea of what he wants to say, and his ideas, as I hope to show, are not those of either the real world where women remained on the whole down-trodden, inferior and abused, nor those of the fantasy world of many of his contemporaries where adultery or fornication were the norm. It is quite certain that Chrétien was strongly opposed to adultery. Instead he puts forward his own ideas, a daring thing for a medieval writer to do in an age when no credit was given for originality. Luttrell has shown that Chrétien comes as near as he can to admitting that although he drew on sources, he used them for his own creations.[43] As a professional writer, presumably dependent on his writing for his living and therefore bound to please his patrons, Chrétien used the vocabulary, the ideas and the attitudes which were in vogue at the time, but like all truly great writers he has an extraordinary richness, so that his poems can be interpreted in many ways using the evidence provided by Chrétien.[44] Chrétien himself may not have realised fully just how much he was putting into his romances, but with regard to his treatment of the theme of love, I would suggest that he knew very well what he was doing. When necessary he might disguise his true ideas, but throughout his poetry he is opposed to contemporary, fashionable morality and attitudes, which may help to explain the apparent change of emphasis in *Le Conte du Graal*. By means of a detailed analysis of each of the five Arthurian romances of Chrétien I hope to show that he has a clear concept of love and the morality linked with it and that he does more than just advance the case for the sort of married love which he seems to prefer to describe. By humour, irony and contrast he brings out the failings and the disadvantages of other sorts of love, particularly the adulterous or unmarried love advocated by some of his contemporaries, especially in the form of the passion experienced by Tristan and Iseult.[45] His answers may not always be wholly convincing but such are the tasks which he set himself.

Notes

1. H. Dupin, *La Courtoisie au moyen âge* (Paris, 1931), passim.
2. M. Lazar, *Amour courtois et fin'amors* (Paris, 1964).
3. F. L. Utley, 'Must we abandon the concept of courtly love?', *Medievalia et Humanistica*, 3 (1972), 316-17 and 322.
4. John Moore, 'Love in Twelfth Century France', *Traditio*, 24 (1968), 431.
5. D. W. Robertson, jnr., 'The Concept of Courtly Love as an Impediment to the Understanding of Medieval Texts' in *The Meaning of Courtly Love*, ed. F. X. Newman (Albany, N.Y., 1968), 17.
6. J. Frappier, 'Sur un procès fait à l'amour courtois', *Romania*, 93, (1972), 145-93.
7. C. Luttrell, *The Creation of the first Arthurian Romance* (London, 1974), 56-57.
8. F. L. Utley, op. cit. 322. 'There is not one courtly love, but twenty or thirty of them...'
9. Lazar, op. cit. 14.
10. B. Wind, 'Ce jeu subtil, l'amour courtois' in *Mélanges offerts à Rita Lejeune*, Vol. II (Gembloux, 1969), 1257.
11. R. Boase, *The Origin and Meaning of Courtly Love* (Manchester, 1977).
12. C. Brooke, Introduction in *Medieval Women*, ed. D. Baker (Oxford, 1978), 5.
13. Ibid. 7.
14. M-C Zai, *Les Chansons courtoises de Chrétien de Troyes* (Berne and Frankfurt, 1974), 95.
15. J. Frappier, 'Vues sur les conceptions courtoises dans les littératures d'oc et d'oïl au xiie siècle', *Cahiers de Civilisation médiévale*, 2 (1959), 153.
16. Ibid. 154-56.
17. Lazar, op. cit. 23.

18. Ibid. 12.
19. J. Le Goff, *La Civilisation de l'occident médiéval* (Paris, 1972), 431.
20. Y. Lefevre, *Histoire mondiale de la femme*, Vol.II, ed. P. Grimal, 100.
21. P. Le Gentil, *La Littérature française du moyen âge* (Paris, 1968), 57.
22. J. Ferrante and G. Economou, editors *In Pursuit of Perfection* (Port Washington, N.Y., 1975), 3.
23. J. F. Benton, 'The Court of Champagne as a Literary Center', *Speculum*, 36 (1961), 578. 'The weightiest evidence, therefore, places the author [Andreas] at the royal court.'
24. Ibid. 580.
25. Ibid. 551. 'Andreas Capellanus may have been Countess Marie's chaplain...' This cautious attitude of Benton is rejected by H. A. Kelly who asserts that Andreas was not at Marie's court. *Love and Marriage in the Age of Chaucer.* (Ithaca, 1975), 36.
26. Benton, op. cit. 586-87. 'The question of Marie's Latinity bears on the intended audience of Andreas' *De Amore;* for if Marie could not understand *De Amore* without the help of a translation, there is little reason to think that it was written for her delectation. The obvious audience for a Latin Treatise would be clerics and a few well-educated laymen, who might have found the first two books of *De Amore* amusing rather than instructive.'
27. John Stevens, *Medieval Romance* (London, 1973), 33.
28. Ibid. 32. 'The moral opportunism of this opening paragraph [of Book III] is hard to beat. It certainly does not encourage us to take the pious recantation of Book III very seriously — indeed it does not encourage us to take anything seriously that Andreas has written.'
29. D. W. Robertson, jnr., 'The Subject of the *De Amore* of Andreas Capellanus', *Modern Philology,* 50 (1952-53), 145-61.
30. W. T. H. Jackson, 'The *De Amore* of Andreas Capellanus and the practice of love at court', *Romanic Review,* 49 (1958), 244.
31. Barbara Nelson Sargent, 'A Medieval Commentary on Andreas Capellanus', *Romania,* 94 (1973), 541. 'I can only conclude that, whatever may have been the Chaplain's intentions, the assertions that any and all medieval readers must have found it humorous, as an ironical presentation of the wrong kind of love, and that Drouart de la Vache's comments prove this, do not stand up under examination.'
32. K. Foster, 'Courtly Love and Christianity', *Aquinas Paper* 39 (London, 1963), 6 'Andreas was evidently something of an extremist. He liked to push ideas as far as they would go. . . The tone and allusions of his work make it clear that he wrote within and for a definite aristocratic "set", the countess of Champagne's in fact; and she was one of the greatest ladies of her time. . . Moreover the ideas of Andreas are broadly in harmony with those of the twelfth century troubadours, so far as ideas of any kind are discernible in their lyrics. In this sense, at least, the *De Amore* is certainly a representative document.'
   See notes 25 and 26 and 28 for critics of some of these views.
33. Ibid. 16.

11

34. Lazar, op. cit. 136. 'La *fin'amors* est un amour caché, adultère, dominé par l'appétit de la chair.'
35. Frances and Joseph Gies, *Women in the Middle Ages* (New York, 1978), 46.
36. J-C Payen, *Le Motif du repentir dans la littérature francaise médiévale* (Geneva, 1968), 262. 'Or la chanson de toile nous donne, certainement, de la réalité médiévale une image plus juste que la poésie des trouvères. . . '
37. Ibid. 263. 'Peut-être autant que l'art raffiné des trouvères la chanson de toile a contribué à éveiller le public médiéval aux problèmes du cœur.'
38. Lucienne Carasso-Bulow, *The Merveilleux in Chrétien de Troyes' Romances* (Geneva, 1976), 143.
39. J. Frappier, 'Hermann J. Weigand et son triptyque sur l'amour courtois', *Amour courtois et Table Ronde* (Geneva, 1973), 59.
40. P. Haidu, *Aesthetic Distance in Chrétien de Troyes* (Geneva, 1968), 41, uses the following turns of phrase; 'Chrétien's prejudice in favor of married love. . .' and '. . .his predilection for married love. . .'
41. Ferrante and Economou, op. cit., 159.
42. P. S. Noble, 'Kay the Seneschal in Chrétien de Troyes and his Predecessors', *Reading Medieval Studies*, 1 (1975), 55-70 and 'The Character of Guinevere in the Arthurian Romances of Chrétien de Troyes', *Modern Language Review*, 67 (1972), 524-35.
43. Luttrell, op. cit. 253.
44. Jessie Crosland, *Medieval French Literature* (Oxford, 1956), 120.
45. P. Gallais, *Genèse du roman occidental; essais sur Tristan et Iseut* (Paris, 1974), 59. '*Tristan* doit être nié. *Tristan* est une tentation à laquelle il ne faut pas succomber.'

EREC ET ENIDE

Whatever date is ascribed to *Erec et Enide* it is generally agreed that it is among the earliest of Chrétien's surviving works and that it is the first of the Arthurian romances by Chrétien. It is also clear that Chrétien's treatment of the idea of love in *Erec et Enide* differs from the treatment of love in his later works.[1] It is the only one of his romances in which love develops after the marriage, as in all the other romances at least one of the participants falls in love before there can be any question of marriage or the love is presented as already in existence at the start of the poem. It is also the only romance where the title focusses attention on the couple as opposed to the male partner.

Erec is a young, unattached knight at the court of Arthur serving the Queen, as he has no lady of his own. Sent to avenge the insult to the Queen, perpetrated by Yder and his dwarf, Erec spends the night at the house of the vavassor who is Enide's father. Enide's beauty is so great that it overwhelms Erec;

> Erec d'autre part s'esbahi,
> quant an li si grant biauté vit. (448-49)[2]

and it is not long before her father explains to Erec that he is keeping Enide for a really good match.

> Mes j'atant ancor meillor point,
> que Dex greignor enor li doint,
> que avanture li amaint
> ou roi ou conte qui l'an maint. (529-32)

Erec is, of course, the son of King Lac, although the vavassor does not yet know this. Erec then enquires about the excitement in the town and is told about the prize of the sparrowhawk which Yder has come to claim. This gives Erec his opportunity to seek his revenge, but first he must make sure that he will have suitable armour. It is only after he has acquired all this information, realised that here is his opportunity for revenge, assured himself that he will have the necessary equipment, that Erec takes the next step. He has to have an 'amie' for whom he will claim the sparrowhawk, and Enide is conveniently to hand. He has already been impressed by her beauty.

> Lors dist Erec, que l'esprevier
> vialt par sa fille desresnier,
> car por voir n'i avra pucele
> qui la centiesme part soit bele; (639-42)

He is in fact the answer to her father's prayer.

> mes je vos promet et otroi,
> se vos armes m'aparelliez
> et vostre fille me bailliez
> demain a l'esprevier conquerre,
> que je l'an manrai an ma terre,
> se Dex la victoire m'an done;
> la li ferai porter corone,
> s'iert reîne de dis citez. (658-65)[3]

There is no mention of love, and the vavassor does not see that as an important omission. The match is seen in purely materialistic terms, and no-one considers asking the opinion of the women. Enide and her mother are not consulted. Her father says;

> tot a vostre comandemant
> ma bele fille vos comant. (675-76)

Enide and her mother are both delighted at the news, but Enide's reaction is quite materialistic.

> et bien savoit qu'il seroit rois
> et ele meîsme enoree,
> riche reîne coronee. (688-90)

In other words this is a business arrangement between the two men. Erec needs a beautiful maiden to champion, and the daughter of the vavassor is at hand. Her birth makes it possible for him to marry her, and he is prepared to do this.[4] The vavassor is naturally delighted at the unexpected arrival of exactly the sort of husband for whom he had been hoping. The women see in this match their chance of an escape from poverty. There is perhaps only one unrealistic element in this. Erec did not need to offer marriage, so quickly at any rate, to secure Enide as his 'amie', although he does know that marriage is what the father intends for his daughter. As the son of King Lac Erec could certainly have looked higher than Enide for his bride, and it seems unlikely that the king's son and heir to the throne would be allowed to choose his bride just to please himself on the spur of the moment. With this one reservation the marriage seems to conform to what would have happened in the twelfth century. The marriage was arranged between the families, and the feelings of the actual participants were of little importance. In this case fortunately neither of them is averse to the marriage and indeed both have reason to be pleased; Erec at winning a partner of outstanding beauty and Enide at making an unexpectedly good marriage. They are attracted to one another for a variety of reasons, physical, material, even opportunistic, but there is no question of love at this point, and this must have been true of many twelfth-century (and later) marriages.

Once the combat between Erec and Yder actually starts, there is the first hint of a deepening relationship. Enide does not seem to know the real reason why Erec is fighting Yder. Erec has only said that he does not like him (602). As she sees Erec fighting for her in what is a desperate struggle, she prays for his success and is in tears. Erec sees this as he draws breath and is inspired by it.

> Erec regarde vers s'amie,
> qui molt dolcemant por lui prie;
> tot maintenant qu'il l'ot veüe,
> se li est sa force creüe;
> por s'amor et por sa biauté
> a reprise molt grant fierté; (907-12)

For the first time love is mentioned in regard to their relationship, presumably the love which Erec assumes that Enide feels for him is his inspiration. The idea that the lady inspires her lover is, of course, part of the courtly tradition. It is present in Wace, where it may be taken as showing that Wace was aware of courtly ideas, but the idea of the lover striving to impress the beloved is much older and part of the general tradition of love in literature, so that it does not necessarily indicate that Chrétien was intending to write in a courtly vein. In any case Enide is not Erec's only inspiration. He quickly remembers that he has promised the Queen to avenge her shame and with this two-fold inspiration overcomes Yder. Erec is not yet very much under the influence of love.

At the celebrations which follow the victory, much attention is paid to Erec but relatively little to Enide who is overjoyed with the situation but is clearly of secondary importance.

> et la bele pucele an mis,
> qui tel joie a de son seignor
> c'onques pucele n'ot greignor. (1300-02)

'Seignor' should not be overstressed in this context, but it does indicate quite clearly the relationship. Erec is in charge and informs his host, Enide's father, of his plans. He will marry Enide at Arthur's court and none of the parents will be present. His lady the Queen will dress Enide herself. Enide's cousin and uncle are shocked at the poor figure that Enide will present at court arriving in her shabby old clothes but Erec will not allow them to interfere. Enide is not consulted about this either. Erec obviously means to be the master in his marriage, but he will accept the gift of a beautiful palfrey for Enide, so that she is at least suitably mounted. Enide may be called Erec's *amie* throughout this section but she has no authority, and no doubt this too represents a realistic portrayal of a twelfth-century marriage. At least at first the husband, older than the wife normally, would expect to be very much in command. Erec is polite and in his way kind but it never occurs to him that Enide might have views of her own to express. Enide is still too young and too inexperienced to speak for herself. Besides she is no doubt overawed by Erec and over-whelmed by the excitement of what is happening to her and restrained by the strictness of her upbringing and the gratitude which she must be feeling. She is so poor that the only possession which she has to take away with her is her newly won sparrowhawk.

> Erec chevalche lez le conte
> et delez lui sa bele amie,
> qui l'esprevier n'oblia mie;
> a son esprevier se deporte,
> nule autre richesce n'an porte. (1420-24)

Even this she owes to Erec and so naturally she is prepared to comply with his wishes.

Chrétien has already indicated that Erec was attracted to Enide at first sight because of her outstanding beauty, but the ride to Arthur's court gives Chrétien the opportunity to develop this idea. At last the couple are alone together and Erec has time to study his newly won bride.

> quant plus l'esgarde et plus li plest . . . (1467)

She is just as interested in him.

> mes ne remire mie mains
> la dameisele le vasal
> de boen voel et de cuer leal
> qu'il feisoit li par contançon. (1478-81)

They are both exceptionally good-looking and are naturally drawn to each other, and Chrétien resorts to a well-established idea to describe the beginning of their love.

li uns a l'autre son cuer anble; (1494)

The ride to the King's court at Cardigan although short gives the couple the opportunity to assess each other and feel the first stirrings of passion, although to judge from the emphasis on the physical attractions of Enide in the lines immediately preceding, it is a passion based largely on physical attraction, coupled with gratitude in the case of Enide.

Their arrival at court has been eagerly awaited and causes considerable excitement. Everyone agrees on Enide's outstanding beauty;

sa grant biauté prisent et loent; (1524)

and Erec gives Enide into the Queen's care stressing her poverty and her good family. Again no thought seems to be given to Enide's reaction to this. Erec calls her 'ma pucele et m'amie' (1535) and makes it clear to the Queen that there is no obstacle to their marriage, but that he would not allow her cousin to dress her more fittingly as he wanted only the Queen to do that. The Queen in her reply 'seems very pleased with this gesture, acknowledging her position.

> . . . 'Molt avez bien fait;
> droiz est que de mes robes ait
> et je li donrai boene et bele,
> tot or androit, fresche et novele.' (1563-66)

She treats Enide with great kindness and generosity, and the result of her attentions is that Enide is indisputably the most beautiful lady at the court and so wins the kiss that follows the death of the White Stag. Enide gracefully accepts whatever happens to her at Arthur's court but there is no sign of any independence.[5] She is a well-bred, perhaps shy girl — who blushes when she becomes the object of attention (1712) — who accepts without question the authority of her future husband which has replaced that of her father. There is no further sign that her feelings towards him are developing or indeed that his have moved beyond the stage of physical attraction. This is true of the actual wedding night as well. Chrétien puts considerable stress on the physical longing felt by both parties, using a clear Biblical reference for a very secular purpose.[6]

> Cers chaciez qui de soif alainne
> ne desirre tant la fontainne,
> n'espreviers ne vient a reclain
> si volantiers quant il a fain,

que plus volantiers n'i venissent,
einçois que il s'antre tenissent. (2027-32)
There are few preliminaries as they gaze upon each other,
satisfaction of the eye being an important part of their enjoyment,
kissing serving to increase the pleasure, but, although it is
delicately expressed, Chrétien makes clear what was the most
important part of the night's work.

De l'amor qui est antr'ax deus
fu la pucele plus hardie:
de rien ne s'est acoardie,
tot sofri, que qu'il li grevast;
ençois qu'ele se relevast,
ot perdu le non de pucele;
au matin fu dame novele. (2048-54)

Physical attraction then is the main element in their love so far. As
yet Erec seems to pay very little attention to any other aspect of
Enide. Her opinions are of no interest to him. He is very much in
charge in his marriage, which seems to be a realistic one for the
period with the bonus that the couple are well matched in age and
appearance and find each other very attractive.

This attraction and his physical desire for Enide are what will
cause Erec's descent into sloth.[7]

Mes tant l'ama Eréc d'amors,
que d'armes mes ne li chaloit,
ne a tornoiemant n'aloit. . .
si an fist s'amie et sa drue;[8]
en li a mise s'antendue,
en acoler et an beisier;
ne se quierent d'el aeisier. (2430-38)

Enide is thus more to Erec than just his wife. As his 'amie' and
'drue' she can be considered as the object of his love and devotion,
but she certainly cannot be seen as having the position of the
courtly dame. She has none of the authority that a dame would be
able to exercise. The idea behind amie and drue seems to be that
Erec is so besotted with her that he cannot bear to leave her,
staying in bed with her until after mid-day (2442-43) and avoiding
his responsibilities which he delegates to others by sending his men
to tournaments instead of going himself. It is hinted that his
passion for her is intensely physical too, and there is nothing
courtly about the lack of self-control which he shows in surrender-
ing to his desire. In fact, if the doctrines codified by Andreas

Capellanus are to be accepted, Erec is a sinner against the courtly code which declared that love between husband and wife was impossible, while several Christian theologians would argue that his affection for his wife was adulterous. Chrétien does not give any indication of supporting this latter view but he makes it clear that Erec is to be blamed for his surrender to physical desire. He is not yet mature enough to combine his varying responsibilities.

The relationship between the couple is brought out clearly by their behaviour at this time of crisis. Even at this moment Chrétien stresses the physical aspect of their love.

> boche a boche antre braz gisoient,
> come cil qui molt s'antre amoient. (2473-74)

Enide fears Erec.

> mes sanblant fere n'an osa,
> que ses sire an mal nel preïst
> asez tost, s'ele le deïst. (2466-68)

She has cause as his reaction to her eventual disclosure shows. Her love is shown by her readiness to accept the blame for causing the downfall of Erec (2499-501). His affection is shown by his initial reaction, calling her 'dolce amie chiere', before he has discovered the cause of her distress. Chrétien stresses that Enide is terrified (2520) and tries to prevaricate.[9] Erec's tone changes immediately to the coldly formal 'Dame' and when she still will not tell him, he threatens her (2534). The husband is asserting his authority, and Enide has little choice but to comply. Erec accepts her explanation with dignity but the coldness between them is signalled by the continuing use of the word 'Dame' (2572). Enide is reduced to despair but Chrétien is not explicit about Erec's reactions. He describes what Erec does but gives no explanation.[10] No doubt Erec's *amour propre* is wounded in two ways.[11] He accepts that the criticisms of his behaviour are justified. All his subsequent behaviour suggests that he is hurt that Enide had so little faith in him that he had to bludgeon the explanation out of her. This would serve to strengthen any fears he might have about her love. He would be well aware that a lady, whose knight was no longer worthy of her, was entitled to look elsewhere.[12] Erec might well feel that Enide's reaction to his questions was not the reaction of one who was wholehearted in love.[13] In his anger, much of it directed at himself, he would make no allowances for Enide's timidity and the awe in which she seems to hold him. His immediate reaction is to reassert his authority which Enide accepts unquestioningly and then to test her further.[14] His affection for her still exists, as his instructions to his father on how to treat her should anything prevent his return prove (2721-27), but his anger is clear in the sharp tone in which she is summoned and then rebuked for keeping him waiting. Similarly his instructions to her on how to behave during their journey are delivered in a tone which brooks no opposition and no questions. Erec will allow no challenge to his authority and does not even wish her company. She has hurt him too badly for him to be able to endure her too close to him at that moment. Her distress at this treatment is great, but she accepts that it is her fault. It is his silence indicating his hatred which upsets her.

> mes de ce sui morte et traïe,
> que mes sires m'a anhaïe. (2785-86)

Enide really does love Erec, although there is something spaniel-like about her submissive attitude. The crisis helps her to understand her true feelings.

As a result when the first group of robbers prepare to attack Erec, it does not take her long to decide that it would be cowardly not to warn him of the impending danger.[15] Erec reacts angrily to her disobedience but says that he will pardon her this once but not again. Almost in spite of himself his affection for her overcomes his outraged pride, although he does his best to disguise this from her by speaking so roughly. Pride may be one of the reasons why he chose to make Enide dress herself in her best for his adventure. She is then not only tempting bait, likely to provoke the sort of incidents which will allow Erec to prove himself, but a visible symbol of his status. Be that as it may, his victory over the three robber knights does little to soften him towards Enide.

> Les trois chevax li comandoit
> devant li mener et chacier,
> et molt la prist a menacier
> qu'ele ne soit plus si hardie
> c'un seul mot de la boche die,
> se il ne l'an done congié. (2912-17)

There is no sign here of any further diminution in his anger with the result that when the five knights get ready to attack, it takes Enide a little more time to decide what to do. His threats are still ringing in her ears (2964) but in the end she decides to speak whatever he may do to her. This time, however, she approaches him with a good deal of trepidation, starting with a simple 'Sire', whereas the first time she had gone straight into her warning. It is only when he answers that she explains the position, which Erec had already appreciated, although he was pretending to have seen nothing. Again he answers very roughly accusing her of disrespect.

> et ne por quant tres bien savoie
> que gueres ne me priseiez. (2996-97)

Nevertheless he pardons her again but with renewed threats. Still unsure of himself and of Enide, Erec is showing all the sensitivity of wounded masculine pride, and his love for Enide is not yet fully reawakened. His victory over the five is followed by a very similar scene to his victory over the three. Enide is given the horses and warned not to speak again.

That night Erec tells Enide to sleep while he watches, but she refuses and he is pleased to accept a reversal of the roles which he proposed.

> Erec l'otroie et bel li fu; (3089)

It seems clear from the soliloquy which Enide delivers during her solitary vigil that she is too unhappy and troubled in her mind to sleep. She probably regards this night of wakefulness as partly a penance and partly a proof of her love. She feels guilty for her lack of faith in Erec.

> Savoir pooie sanz dotance
> que tel chevalier ne meillor
> ne savoit l'an de mon seignor. (3104-06)

She blames her troubles on her pride.

> Lasse, fet ele, si mar vi
> mon orguel et ma sorcuidance! (3102-03)

Erec sleeps peacefully throughout the night, suggesting an easier mind than Enide's, although as Enide has pointed out;

> il dormira, qui plus se diaut. (3088)

The visit of the Count suggests that Erec is already beginning to recover a little of his confidence, as he makes no objection when the Count asks permission to sit next to Enide. Erec has no wish to assume the role of the despised jealous husband.

> Erec ne fu mie jalous,
> que il n'i pansa nule boise; (3296-97)

Both Erec and Enide display irreproachable manners in this scene, as when the Count sits beside her;

> devers lui se torna la dame
> qui molt estoit saige et cortoise. (3306-07)

Chrétien is indicating that Enide is above suspicion and knows how to conduct herself, probably nothing more. The Count offers very flattering terms to Enide and also indicates that he has sensed the strain in the marriage.

> bien voi et sai que vostre sire
> ne vos ainme ne ne vos prise; (3322-23)

Enide rejects the Count in vigorous terms which serve only to increase his ardour and turn him to threats, so that she has to resort to guile to outmanoeuvre him. She does it with one motive;

> por son seignor fu delivrer. (3409)

and watches the whole night so as to protect Erec who is still quite unsuspecting, which indicates a certain degree of trust on his part. Like a 'bone dame et leax' Enide rouses Erec in time to make their escape together, and Erec realises that she has proved herself.

> Or ot Erec que bien se prueve
> vers lui sa fame lëaumant; (3480-81)

Nevertheless he still forbids Enide to warn him of any impending danger which she may see, but as soon as she hears the noise of the Count's pursuit, she has to warn him. His reaction is as angry as ever so that when the couple have escaped from the Count, Enide is frightened of warning Erec about Guivret because he has threatened her so much. This time she really has great difficulty in bringing herself to warn Erec, but she realises that she must save him from death.

> Ele li dit; il la menace;
> mes n'a talant que mal li face,
> qu'il aparçoit et conuist bien
> qu'ele l'ainme sor tote rien,
> et il li tant que plus ne puet. (3751-55)

In other words Erec has now accepted that Enide truly loves him and realises that he loves her, but he is not yet ready to show this to her. He is still keeping up the appearance of anger, carrying out his word for she had disobeyed him yet again, and preserving his authority.

Enide plays no part in the scene with Guivret nor does she have any say in the matter of whether or not they go to Arthur's court. Erec does not consult her, nor does she offer an opinion unasked. It is the same the next morning. Erec decides that they are leaving, and Enide obediently accepts his decision. A sign that his anger has cooled, however, is the fact that before he goes to the aid of the *amie* of Cadoc, he does tell Enide what he is going to do, and as before she unquestioningly accepts his plan. Another sign of his increasing love for her is his anxiety to return after the adventure.

> Et il restoit an grant redot
> qu'aucuns ne l'an eüst menee,
> qui l'eüst a sa loi tornee;
> si se hastoit molt del retor. (4548-51)

His apparent death, when he swoons as his wounds reopen, brings out the full extent of Enide's love for him as she raves over his body and eventually resolves to commit suicide, but she is prevented from committing this sin by the opportune arrival of the Comte de Limors. Her love is now to be tested in another way as the Comte is anxious to marry her and prepared to use violence to achieve his ends if necessary. She is forced through a marriage ceremony, and the Comte's attitude is probably typical of many twelfth-century husbands. His vassals rebuke him for striking Enide but he will have none of it.

> Teisiez vos an tuit! fet li cuens;
> la dame est moie et je sui suens,
> si ferai de li mon pleisir. (4799-801)

When Enide refutes this, swearing that she will never be his, he strikes her again. The contrast with the behaviour of Erec, even at his angriest, is marked. It is at this point that Erec recovers and kills the Comte so that he and Enide are able to escape, and their reconciliation is complete.

> Et Erec, qui sa fame an porte,
> l'acole et beise et reconforte; (4879-80)

He follows his gestures with words.

> . . . c'or vos aim plus qu'ainz mes ne fis,
> et je resui certains et fis
> que vos m'amez parfitemant.
> Or voel estre d'or en avant,
> ausi con j'estoie devant,
> tot a vostre comandemant;
> et se vos rien m'avez mesdit,
> je le vos pardoing tot et quit
> del forfet et de la parole. (4885-93)

Erec is now certain that they do both love each other. Enide has been tested in every possible way and has never been found wanting. He has proved his worth to her and to himself and any doubts that he may have harboured have been settled. As a result he can say that he loves her more than ever, because he now appreciates her as a woman and as his wife, and she is no longer just the object of his physical desire. He no longer suspects that her love for him wavered because of his lapse into *recreantise* and he is prepared to be as before *tot a vostre comandemant*. If he really means that he is going to behave as before, *tot a vostre comandemant* can only be a polite form of words, because Erec has never been at Enide's *comandemant*. He has never even consulted her or asked for her advice, let alone obeyed any order of hers. It is not a sign of a courtly submission on his part.[16] It is an expression of the nature of his love for her but one which they both interpret in the light of their past relationship. The next three lines confirm Erec's dominance. He is prepared to forgive Enide, and the reader should not be surprised because it has been made clear that Enide too regards herself as guilty of pride and doubting her husband. Erec can be magnanimous now that all doubts have been removed, but there can be no argument as to which is the dominant partner in the marriage. Enide is only too happy to accept a reconciliation on Erec's terms.

Just when her happiness has been restored, it looks as if Enide will lose it again when Erec is overcome by Guivret. Enide rushes to his aid filled with grief, but the incident turns out for the best, as the wounded Erec can be cared for in Guivret's castle, where Enide is able to prove her devotion again by tending him herself (5092-95). Even when he is under the care of Guivret's sisters who are far more skilled in medicine than Enide, she will scarcely leave his side.

> mes, qui qu'alast ne anz ne hors,
> toz jorz estoit devant son cors
> Enyde, cui plus an tenoit. (5167-69)

With the return of Erec to health Enide recovers her beauty which worry had spoiled, and they are able to recover the happiness of their honeymoon period. Again Chrétien is quite explicit about the physical satisfaction which both enjoy.

> Ansanble jurent an un lit,
> et li uns l'autre acole et beise;
> riens nule n'est qui tant lor pleise.
> Tant ont eü mal et enui,
> il por li et ele por lui,
> c'or ont feite lor penitance.
> Li uns ancontre l'autre tance
> comant il li puise pleisir;
> del sorplus me doi bien teisir.

24

> Or ont lor dolor obliee
> et lor grant amor afermee,
> que petit mes lor an sovient. (5200-11)

Their love for each other and their enjoyment of this love are
clear, but Chrétien also indicates that they have both suffered
considerably and done penance, suggesting that both are to blame
for the suffering. As a result of this suffering it seems clear that
they love each other more deeply and with greater understanding
than they did before.[17] Both are prepared to put all their troubles
behind them, but they are wiser and more understanding as the
result of their suffering, and their love is the stronger for it. The
saddle, which Enide is given with the story of Dido and Eneas
worked upon it (5289-98), may point the contrast between the
tragic love of the Carthaginian Queen, betrayed and deserted by
her lover, and the happy, conjugal love of Erec and Enide, but if
that is Chrétien's intention it is left implicit. The moral is not
drawn openly.

Chrétien does, however, make a much more explicit contrast
between different sorts of relationship in the next episode where
Erec defeats Mabonagrain. Again Erec does not consult Enide
about this adventure, and although she spends the night in great
distress (5628-33), she does not attempt to intervene. She accepts
that in matters of this sort she has no standing. Erec takes an
affectionate leave of her, and the change in their relationship for
the better is clear. He calls her 'bele, douce suer' and 'gentix dame
lëax et sage' (5783-84) and rebukes her gently for fearing the
unknown on his behalf. He does not see this as a lack of confidence
in him but accepts it as proof of her love. To comfort her he
reminds her that love of her gives him courage.

> car bien sachiez seüremant,
> s'an moi n'avoit de hardemant
> fors tant con vostre amors m'an baille,
> ne crienbroie je an bataille,
> cors a cors, nul home vivant. (5805-09)

He is not boasting when he says this, but thinking of her peace of
mind, and this is a new element in Erec, this consideration for
Enide. Not only is he no longer solely concerned with his own
glory (he is after all undertaking an adventure which is more likely
to end in defeat than not, and his motivation seems to be altruistic
not selfish), he is actually considering Enide and her feelings which
he has not done hitherto. With her inspiration to help him he

overcomes Mabonagrain after a brutal struggle which ends in a somewhat unknightly grappling match, because Mabonagrain is not equally inspired by his lady. He admits that his slavery was distasteful to him from the start, although he did not dare reveal it.

Des que ge soi le boen et vi
a la rien que ge oi plus chiere,
n'an dui feire sanblant ne chiere
que nule rien me despleüst; (6032-35)

He also describes the joy which will be caused by his release from this bondage (6068-70). Mabonagrain has been the victim of a courtly relationship. He and his lady were not married, he served her patiently and was obedient to her slightest whim. The result was that it was easy for her to trap him into this prison, cutting him off from society and leading a life which was positively harmful, as the heads of the dead knights prove. Chrétien may be ridiculing the love suggested by the troubadours by taking it to its logical and extreme conclusion.[18] Instead of the love benefiting society, it had become a scourge, and what had started as a courtly relationship with the knight serving his lady has been perverted by the lack of *mesure* on the part of the lady who selfishly determines to control her lover.[19] Mabonagrain's defeat symbolises Chrétien's condemnation of this selfishness. Society's disapproval is also made clear by the general joy which is felt at the ending of the adventure of the *Joie de la Cort*.[20]

Enide thoughtfully goes to console the *amie* of Mabonagrain who is far from pleased at the outcome of the combat as she fears the loss of her lover. She describes her secret love affair with Mabonagrain, an account which does not quite tally with his and which puts her in a far more favourable light as only complying with his wishes, and her love affair contrasts strikingly with Enide's which was conducted openly and honorably

—Bele cosine, il m'espousa,
si que mes peres bien le sot
et ma mere qui joie en ot.
Tuit le sorent et lié an furent
nostre parant, si com il durent; (6242-46)

Enide's match was recognised by society and approved by her family, thus conforming to twelfth-century conventions, while her cousin's elopement was secret, cutting the participants off from society. Enide understands very well the nature of her love for Erec and his for her.

Il m'ainme molt, et je lui plus,
tant qu'amors ne puet estre graindre. (6254-55)
The greatness of her love is due to her gratitude for he has raised
her from poverty to royal status. Erec, of course, is not similarly
obligated to Enide, and so her love is the greater. This has been
shown through their adventures, for it took much longer for Erec's
love to develop from his first physical passion, whereas the
beginning of the crisis had forced Enide to assess her attitude
earlier. She is content with her position because in twelfth-century
terms she is lucky to have the love of her husband and realising
that she owes him everything, she loves him 'tant qu'amors ne puet
estre graindre' as she says. His love gives her confidence. She has
not the authority nor the force of character of a Guinevere who
will advise her husband unasked, but Enide is now able to take
decisions for herself and to act independently in her own sphere,
as her decision to comfort her cousin shows. She is now ready to be
crowned as the queen consort of Erec at Nantes, where, although
her role is naturally of secondary importance, she is recognised as
a worthy partner for Erec.

It must be evident from this survey that the relationship between
Erec and Enide is in no way courtly.[21] The vocabulary used in the
poem, *amie, dame, a vostre comandemant* is superficially courtly,
but the spirit behind the words is not. Erec is the dominant partner
throughout, and Enide accepts this unquestioningly. She blames
herself for his *recreantise* and accepts without demur his forgiveness when for the modern reader it is hard to see where she has
erred. Her fault lies in doubting Erec, and once Erec has
appreciated that she doubts his worth, he is immediately suspi-
cious of her. Hence his harshness and his determination to test her
to the limit. Her love survives this ordeal, and Erec is convinced of
her fidelity and her devotion so that his own love for her is not only
reawakened but is strengthened and deepened. They mature from
a young couple hedonistically enjoying the delights of their
honeymoon,[22] with no thought for others or for their responsibilities, to a wiser couple, just as passionately in love and finding just
as much enjoyment in their love but with more control so that they
are able to think of others and to use their talents for the benefit of
others. In this way they become ready for the roles of king and
queen to which the death of Erec's father will shortly call them.

It seems probable that Chrétien is presenting this concept of
conjugal love as an ideal,[23] because their relationship is contrasted

with the sterile, but apparently courtly relationship of Mabonagrain and Enide's cousin, the effects of which are wholly harmful.[24]
Mabonagrain won his lady through service, serves her loyally,
obeys her slightest wish, but her lack of *mesure* makes her selfishly
isolate them from society and her lack of confidence in her lover
shows in the means which she uses to keep him by her side. The
confidence of Enide, who is married, in her husband is in marked
contrast. Again the illicit relationship of Dido and Eneas is
mentioned in a way which suggests a contrast between their
unhappy affair and the happy resolution of the troubles of Erec
and Enide. The two counts show by their behaviour how lucky
Enide is to have found a husband like Erec, for there is a distinct
note of realism in their treatment of Enide. Chrétien's argument
is, however, that the love which Erec and Enide feel for each other
is sufficient to withstand all their troubles, both external and
between themselves. This love is the force which turns them from
a selfishly inward looking couple to a mature, responsible
couple,[25] who are to be admired by all. The relationship between
them is clear. The man is dominant, and the woman is happy to
accept her role, but the man must not abuse his authority,[26] and it
is because she has confidence in his love that the woman is happy
to accept her role. Erec and Enide are an ideal couple physically
and so their relationship has become an ideal,[27] but Chrétien is
suggesting how much good there is for everyone in such a
relationship,[28] as compared with the other relationships or types of
behaviour which he mentions. Love properly used can be a force
for positive good in society but when abused as by Enide's cousin
its effects are to be deplored.[29]

Notes

1. Lazar, op. cit. 207. '*Erec* n'est pas encore un roman *courtois* du même
   niveau que les autres romans de Chrétien. Il est à mi-chemin entre
   l'*Eneas* et le *Cligès.*' See also E. Köhler, *L'Aventure chevaleresque*,
   tr. E. Kaufholz (Paris, 1974), 168. 'L'attitude d'Erec à l'égard
   d'Enide est tout autre que courtoise. . .' Lazar sees in *Erec* values
   close to those of the *chansons de geste,* a view supported by R.
   Michener, 'Courtly Love in Chrétien de Troyes; the *demande
   d'amour*', *Studia Neophilologica*, 42 (1970), 355.
2. All quotations are from *Les Romans de Chrétien de Troyes*, I, Erec et
   Enide, ed. M. Roques, CFMA, 80 (Paris, 1952).

28

3. M. Lot-Borodine, *La Femme et l'amour au xiie siècle d'après les poèmes de Chrétien de Troyes* (Paris, 1909), 31. 'Dans toute son attitude on sent déjà le seigneur et maître.'
4. Ibid. 33, 'Erec, lui aussi, déclare qu'Enide est son égale. . .'
5. W. T. H. Jackson, 'Faith unfaithful; the German reaction to courtly love', in *The Meaning of Courtly Love*, ed. F. X. Newman (Albany, 1968), 56. 'It is oversimplifying her character to describe her as a "simple, unsophisticated girl who is unaffected by courtly trappings".' Maura Coghlan makes the point with greater force. M. Coghlan, 'The Flaw in Enide's Character', *Reading Medieval Studies*, 5 (1979), 26. 'She has been bred for years to a complete self-assurance. . .'
6. Marcelle Thiébaux, *The Stag of Love* (Ithaca & London, 1974), 114. 'Chrétien's allusions to animals of the hunt here point to an incomplete union, which is what the events of the romance also go on to reveal.'
7. Luttrell, op. cit. 61. 'Erec has made his marriage a voluptuous condition, and with this abuse he becomes a Paris, that symbol of the warrior whose spirit is broken by love, and who ruined by Venus' fire takes love-making to be his war.'
8. M. Lot-Borodine, op. cit. 37, takes this as a compliment. 'Chrétien met en lumière ici, comme on le voit, la compatibilité du mariage avec la passion amoureuse. L'épouse est aussi en même temps "l'amie" du chevalier.' Luttrell, op. cit. 60, disagrees, and in view of what follows in the poem he is the more convincing. 'By this phrase Chrétien means to indicate that Erec treats Enide like a paramour. With inordinate love gone is propriety. . .'
9. E. S. Sheldon, 'Why does Chrétien's Erec treat Enide so harshly?' *Romanic Review*, 5 (1914), 115-26. Sheldon claims that Enide's timidity and prevarication make her responsible for Erec doubting her love. Thus she brings the hardship on herself.
10. Chrétien may be using animal symbolism to make one of his points. Erec sits on a rug with 'l'image d'un lieupart', indicating his return to valour, but not yet to its highest degree, which would be symbolised by a lion. J. Frappier, 'Pour le commentaire d'*Erec et Enide*', *Marche Romane*, 20 (1970), 29, examines this in detail.
11. Z. P. Zaddy, 'Pourquoi Erec se décide-t-il à partir en voyage avec Enide?' *Cahiers de Civilisation médiévale*, 7 (1964), 184. '. . . l'amour-propre, et ses exigences, explique tout dans la conduite d'Erec.'
12. Barbara Nelson Sargent-Baur, 'Erec's Enide: "sa fame ou s'amie"?', *Romance Philology*, 33 (1980), 379. 'Not only would the *fame* or *amie* of such an unsatisfactory lover be justified in withdrawing her favour, . . . she ought to withdraw it.'
13. E. Hoepffner, ' "Matière et sens" dans le roman d'*Erec et Enide*', *Archivum Romanicum*, 18 (1934), 443, seems to misinterpret this episode. '. . . la dureté d'Erec. . . c'est un jeu cruel mais nécessaire pour éprouver la force de cet amour.' Erec is not playing. For him the game is over, as the change of tone shows. This also seems to me to cast doubt on Brogyanyi's interpretation. G. J. Brogyanyi, 'Motiva-

tion in *Erec et Enide'*, *Kentucky Romance Quarterly*, 19 (1972), 417. '. . . vengeance and anger are not Erec's leading motives in subjecting Enide to the trials of the adventures. His main purpose is didactic. . .' Erec is angry, and his didactic purpose, if any, is to teach Enide a lesson.

14. Barbara Nelson Sargent-Baur, op. cit. 384-85, argues that courtly love (with the lady dominant) was accepted as a game. Erec is prepared to play the game *until* real life becomes too demanding. Enide has challenged his authority, and so the game is over.

15. This indicates that Enide is quite capable of exercising her own judgement, at least when it is a question of Erec's, and indeed her own, safety. She is driven to speak by her fear that silence would be cowardly (implicitly beneath a lady of her rank) as Maura Coghlan shows, op. cit. 31. This suggests that Marie-Noelle Lefay-Toury has not noticed the change taking place in Enide when she describes her; 'Enide entièrement soumise à son mari et qui n'agit qu'en fonction de lui.' M-N Lefay-Toury, 'Roman breton et mythes courtois', *CCM*, 15 (1972), 193.

16. D. Kelly, 'La forme et le sens de la quête dans l'*Erec et Enide* de Chrétien de Troyes', *Romania*, 92 (1971), 350, would not agree. '. . . Erec se soumet de nouveau à la domination de sa femme. Leur amour est redevenu courtois.' This seems to overlook the context in which Erec is speaking.

17. J. Stevens, op. cit. 38. 'The reconciliation of Erec and Enide after their period of miserable estrangement is truly romantic in feeling: they are renewed with all the freshness of new love.'

18. L. Pollmann, *Die Liebe in der hochmittelalterlichen Literatur Frankreichs* (Frankfurt, 1966), 88. 'Chrétien de Troyes ist offensichtlich bemüht, in Form einer Parodie die Unterordnung des Mannes unter die Frau, wie sie die Trobadors bekennen, ad absurdum zu führen, als vom Standpunkt des höfisch-ritterlichen Denkens unhaltbar.'

19. E. Hoepffner, op. cit. 448. 'La véritable opposition pour Chrétien est donc entre les deux femmes, entre Enide et la dame du verger. A l'amour intéressé de l'une l'auteur oppose l'amour égoïste et tyrannique de l'autre.' Lot-Borodine, op. cit. 74. 'Ainsi le désintéressement si pur de la femme d'Erec est mis pleinement en lumière par l'égoïsme intense de l'amie de Mabonagrain.'

20. Luttrell, op. cit. 65. 'The form of courtly love that had non-marital relations exerted fascination on Chrétien's contemporaries, and that it was so attractive makes its picture the climax of Erec's adventure and the greatest danger of all.' In other words this is the greatest test for Erec.

21. Ferrante, op. cit. 144-45. 'Even in *Erec* Chrétien reverses the normal courtly relationships; when the man becomes aware of his own imperfections he withdraws from his lady, tests her and eventually restores his favour to her.' This is typical of the depth of Chrétien's approach in that he is able to combine the ridiculing of a literary convention with realistic characterisation and a very plausible twelfth century situation.

22. M. Payen, *Les Origines de la courtoisie dans la littérature française médiévale*, II, Le Roman, Centre de Documentation Universitaire (Paris, 1967), 28. 'Leur amour, d'abord presqu' exclusivement sensuel, devient peu à peu, un amour adulte, fondé sur la générosité tout autant que sur le désir.'

23. R. R. Bezzola, *Le sens de l'aventure et de l'amour* (Paris, 1947), 78-79, rejects this view, but his reasoning is not based on adequate proof.

24. Lot-Borodine, op. cit. 74. 'On dirait presque que Chrétien oppose ici l'idée même du foyer à celle d'une libre union, fondée uniquement sur l'égoïsme.' Even more telling are the views of A. Press, 'Le Comportement d'Erec envers Enide dans le roman de Chrétien de Troyes', *Romania*, 90 (1969), 534. 'Le contraste établi au cours de cet entretien, et qui oppose le comportement de ce couple à celui de Maboagrain et de son amie, suggère d'abord, que pour Chrétien, seul l'amour qui s'épanouit dans la société ouvertement et sans contrainte, et qui par là contribue à la joie de la société tout entière, peut mener au bonheur. Par contre, l'amour secret, caché. . . n'est qu'une source constante de méfiance et d'angoisse et n'aboutit qu'à l'échec.'

25. R. Michener, op. cit. 354, would not take this view. 'Chrétien was not yet inclined to portray love as the crucial factor in human existence. . .' Michener sees the poem as a clash between the values of epic and the values of courtly love with the former triumphing. The text does not seem to support this interpretation, as the whole atmosphere with its stress on the individual and the woman is quite different from that associated with epic. See also D. Kelly, op. cit. 340, for the opposite view. 'C'est enfin l'amour qui donne à chaque aventure une signification particulière. . .'

26. This view persisted for many centuries in aristocratic circles. Marguerite de Navarre, *l'Heptaméron*, ed. M. François (Paris, 1960), Nouvelle 37, 269.

27. Hoepffner, op. cit. 449, 'L'amour conjugal fait d'une part du dévouement total de la femme, toujours prête à se sacrifier pour son époux, fait d'autre part de l'amour protecteur du mari qui trouve dans ce sentiment même les sources profondes de son héroïsme chevaleresque.' This is true as far as it goes but the couple have progressed to understanding their duty and their role in society as well.

28. P. Le Gentil, op. cit. 86, brings out the importance of the couple and its social role. '. . . Erec et Enide conquièrent la *Joie*, une joie qui est la leur, mais illumine en même temps la société courtoise toute entière.'

29. S. Gallien, *La Conception sentimentale de Chrétien de Troyes* (Paris, 1975), 36. 'Donc, dès son premier roman, Chrétien est réfractaire à la conception courtoise de l'amour, notamment l'adultère.' Adultery is implicitly condemned by the celebration of marriage but there is no adulterous relationship in this poem. Neither Mabonagrain nor his lady is married.

CLIGÉS

In *Erec et Enide* Chrétien seems to be proving the worth of married love in a traditional marriage. The love is tested and strengthened by the differences between the partners which are resolved, and it is contrasted with other less satisfactory types of love, which are shown to be harmful to the lovers as well as to society in general. In *Cligés* which is generally accepted as being the romance which he wrote next after *Erec et Enide* his purpose is quite different. The many references, mostly disparaging, to the Tristan legend and to the behaviour of Iseult in particular, the plot and the structure of the story all confirm that it is a refutation of the Tristan legend.[1] Chrétien seems to have a horror of adultery, particularly when one woman is loved by two men, for it is Iseult whose behaviour is most frequently cited. In one way the fact that the romance is written with such a clear purpose, to show up the deficiencies of the Tristan legend and to deplore the type of behaviour illustrated by it, makes the interpretation of love in *Cligés* slightly easier. The relationship between the characters is less subtle than in *Erec et Enide,* because it is not the only feature which engages the author's close attention. In *Erec et Enide* the relationship between the characters develops and vitally affects the plot, because it provides the motivation for some of Erec's actions. The relationship is also affected by incidents in the plot as Erec and Enide view each other in a different light as a result of what happens. There is relatively little of this in *Cligés,* where the main problems are declaring the love for the beloved and then consummating the affair.

As in the Tristan story the first part of the romance is devoted to the love of Cligés' parents, Alexander and Soredamors. They are both young, beautiful, of royal birth and very much in love. There is in fact absolutely no reason why they should not get married to general rejoicing. Neither, however, has the courage to declare his or her love, nor it would seem the wit to indicate it covertly to the beloved. Their relationship shows a blend of Ovidian and courtly influences.[2]

They cannot sleep, they grow pale and weary, which the Queen attributes to the effects of the sea voyage, and spend their nights in lengthy soliloquies philosophising on the nature of love and their particular problems. Alexander, like a courtly lover, shows timidity, is prepared to serve his lady, is made happy by the merest token from her and is so terrified of displeasing her that he cannot take advantage of the most favourable opportunities.[3]

> Li rois . . .
> Et si li dit bien et afiche
> Qu'il n'a nule chose tant chiere,
> Se il fet tant qu'il la requiere,
> Fors la corone et la reïne,
> Que il ne l'an face seisine.
> Alixandres de ceste chose
> Son desirrier dire n'en ose,
> Et bien set qu'il n'i faudroit mie,
> Se il li requeroit s'amie.
> Tant crient que il ne depleüst
> Celi qui grant joie en eüst . . . (2180-92)[4]

Soredamors, on the other hand, does not seek at all to play the role of the courtly *dompna*. She has no desire to dominate Alexander and to control him. She has no wish to make him wait and serve patiently, because she is very much in love with him.[5] As a result she is partly occupied with the nature of her love, as this is a new experience for her and she had hitherto resisted love,

> Qui desdaigneuse estoit d'amors; (440)

and partly with thoughts of the beloved, although like many lovers her love is self-centred, and she is more concerned with her own suffering at first.[6] As each of the lovers longs for the other but is too timid to take the first step, Soredamors because she believes that Alexander is not in love with her;

> Ja ne me prie il ne requiert;
> Amerai le ge, s'il ne m'aimme? (484-85)

while Alexander does not dare to address her;

> Mes celi don plus li remanbre
> N'ose aparler, ne aresnier. (574-75)

they have to suffer in silence and to be satisfied with feasting their eyes upon each other. Because they have to repress their love, they find that it grows ever more intense, and both of them find pleasure in the anguish which they undergo.

> Je ne quier que cist max me lest. (860)

says Alexander while Soredamors also comments;

> Or me grieve ce que je voi.
> Grieve? Nel fet, ençois me siet,
> Et se ge voi rien qui me griet,
> Don n'ai ge mes ialz an baillie? (472-75)

Because of their excessive timidity there is no reason why their silent suffering should ever come to an end, since Chrétien is clearly not going to parallel the irregular affair of Rivalen and Blancheflor in the Tristan legend. Soredamors is far too strictly brought up to consent to any irregularity. She is prepared to try to encourage Alexander;

> Or del sofrir tant que je voie
> Si jel porroie metre an voie
> Par sanblant et par moz coverz.
> Tant ferai qu'il an sera cerz
> De m'amor, se requerre l'ose. (1031-35)

but she finds this very difficult as her debate on whether to use the term 'ami' to him shows. Alexander on the other hand is so afraid of displeasing her, that he cannot even make use of the opportunities which are presented to him. This is very different from the behaviour of *Erec et Enide* where it is taken for granted that the girl will be only too pleased to be married to a suitable husband, and no-one even thinks of consulting her. Alexander is a much more courtly lover than Erec.

Fortunately for the lovers the Queen realises that they are in love and takes the initiative in solving their dilemma. Without her intervention as a sort of *dea ex machina* it is hard to see how they would have resolved their problem. As it is, they are married with all possible haste to general rejoicing. Although Alexander adopts a very courtly tone when replying to the admonitions of the Queen;

> S'ele de li rien ne m'otroie,
> Totevoies m'otroi a li. (2290-91)

the Queen's comments on love are much more practical and do not support the courtly idea of concealment and suffering. She is an outspoken advocate of the advantages of marriage (there seems to be no irony intended, as Chrétien has not yet made the Queen the leading adulteress of the court, and his audience may not have been familiar with the Celtic legends of her adultery).[7]

> De ce trop folemant ovrez
> Que chascuns son panser ne dit,

> Qu'au celer li uns l'autre ocit;
> D' Amors omecide serez.
> Or vos lo que ja ne querez
> Force ne volanté d'amor.
> Par mariage et par enor
> Vos antre aconpaigniez ansanble;
> Ensi porra, si com moi sanble,
> Vostre amors longuemant durer. (2260-69)

This, of course, forcefully contradicts one of the main tenets of Andreas Capellanus, if one takes him seriously, but it is very much in keeping with Chrétien's ideas, as seen in *Erec*, that love within marriage is the ideal solution.

Alexander and Soredamors then provide an idealised introduction to the love affair of their son Cligés, since for them everything is resolved for the best, and the only obstacles to their love affair are of their own making and caused by their excessive modesty and timidity.[8] Theirs is very much a partnership. Alexander seeks to serve Soredamors, and this does not seem to be just a turn of phrase, as it was in *Erec et Enide*, but to judge from his behaviour before their marriage, he is genuinely considerate and thoughtful. Soredamors also does not seek to dominate and comes to Alexander without hesitation, the moment it is fitting for her to do so. In the depiction of their love Chrétien has blended together a variety of influences and yet under the elaborate imagery and idealised setting has preserved a recognisable picture of the growing love of two young people, which could happen. As in *Erec et Enide* realism is not totally absent.

With Cligés and Fénice the case is very different. Fénice is engaged to Cligés' uncle Alis before she sees Cligés and so, although they fall in love on sight, it is already too late. Their love cannot be innocent and untroubled in the way that the love of Alexander and Soredamors was. Chrétien takes great pains to make it clear that Alis is entirely to blame as he is perjuring himself by taking a wife at all, but this is of no help to the young couple. They are so beautiful that their love is immediate. The physical attraction is so powerful that Fénice falls in love although she does not know who Cligés is. They do not realise that the other returns their love as their eyes effect the exchange of hearts for them.

> Ses ialz et son cuer i a mis,
> Et cil li ra son cuer promis. (2777-78)

Unlike Tristan, with whom Cligés has just been compared to his
advantage, no potion is necessary to bring about the love between
the two young people. From the very beginning Cligés is inspired
by the thought of Fénice and strives to win her approbation.

Et cil por li se retravaille
Del behorder apertemant,
Por ce qu'ele oie seulemant
Que il est preuz et bien adroiz. (2874-77)

Fénice has no intention of not following her love but realises that
this will require some guile.

Mes par force avoir li estuet
Celui qui pleire ne li puet; (2947-48)

At this point she is lucky in that she is able to secure the services of
Thessala, her nurse, who is able to provide a potion which will
enchant Alis and leave him with the impression but not the reality
of his enjoyment of Fénice. The parallel with the Tristan legend is
clear, but, of course, the purpose of the potion is quite different.
No mistake is made in administering it to Alis (ironically Cligés
unwittingly hands it to him),[9] and in this way Fénice is able to
avoid the fate of Iseult which is her main purpose.

Mialz voldroie estre desmanbree
Que de nos deus fuşt remanbree
L'amors d'Ysolt et de Tristan,
Don mainte folie dit an,
Et honte en est a reconter. (3105-9)

Through Fénice Chrétien is expressing his distaste for the
adulterous relationship of the Tristan legend and also for the
adultery associated with courtly love. The triangle in *Cligés* is
eminently suitable for courtly love, as a young married woman
with an elderly husband is in love with a young unmarried knight
who returns her love and is prepared to serve her as she deserves.
Fénice alone is responsible for the refusal to permit a courtly
relationship, as she is determined that she will never allow herself
to be loved by two men. Her condemnation of Iseult's behaviour is
scathing.

Ja ne m'i porroie acorder
A la vie qu'Isolz mena.
Amors en li trop vilena,
Que ses cuers fu a un entiers,
Et ses cors fu a deus rentiers.
Ensi tote sa vie usa

N'onques les deus ne refusa. (3110-16)

Fénice's philosophy is summed up by the famous line

Qui a le cuer, cil a le cors . . . (3123)[10]

This is also a protest against arranged marriages, for Fénice realises that she cannot resist her father's decision, nor, once she is married, can anyone else intervene between husband and wife, however her future husband treats her. There is no easy solution to her problem, and Chrétien resorts to the magic potion of Thessala to secure an escape for Fénice. The potion is acceptable as part of the story, because Chrétien is following the Tristan legend in which a different potion had an important role at a similar point in the story, but its use here serves to underline the impossibility of the dilemma facing Fénice. In real life there was no easy solution to what must have been a not uncommon situation as long as arranged matches existed. Either the bride forgot her real love or she settled for an adulterous affair. It was, to say the least, improbable that she could preserve herself for her lover.

Once Fénice has succeeded in deceiving Alis thanks to Thessala's potion, she has to let Cligés know what she has done, and this she intends to do from the beginning. Fénice has every expectation and intention of becoming Cligés' lover.

Car par ce cuidera venir

A sa joie, que que il tart,

Que ja tant n'iert de male part

Cligés, s'il set que ele l'aint,

Que por li grant joie ne maint,

(Garder cuide son pucelage

Por lui sauver son heritage)

Qu'il aucune pitié n'en ait,

S'a boene nature retrait

Et s'il est tex com estre doit. (3180-89)

Her motives are presented as altruistic. She knows that Alis has perjured himself by marrying her, and by preserving her virginity she will preserve Cligés' heritage, but this is not the real reason. Fénice is consumed by love, just like Iseult, but as she is more in control of herself than Iseult and has fewer opportunities to satisfy her desire, she can both wait for her physical satisfaction and consider how best to preserve her reputation. The couple share the timidity of Alexander and Soredamors but with better cause as their love cannot be innocent. Neither of them, as yet, has any

reason to suppose that his (or her) love is returned, and therefore
both are afraid to make the first move in case they are rebuffed.
Even when Cligés has rescued Fénice from the Saxon kidnappers
he does not speak; nor does she.

> Mes tant criement le refuser
> Qu'il n'osent lor cuers ancuser. (3781-2)

Their eyes tell the truth, but they cannot interpret these messages.
Chrétien seems to approve of this behaviour on the part of Fénice.

> Se cele comancier ne l'ose,
> N'est mervoille, car sinple chose
> Doit estre pucele et coarde. (3793-5)

She is behaving as she ought to, and her behaviour is in keeping
with her determination to preserve her reputation. He feels it
necessary to explain that fear is an essential part of love;

> Qui amer vialt, crienbre l'estuet,
> Ou autrement amer ne puet; (3855-56)

so that Cligés is behaving exactly as he should, but Chrétien adds
that Cligés would have spoken were it not for the fact that Fénice
is his uncle's wife. Clearly propriety plays at least as large a role as
the fear caused by love in motivating Cligés' behaviour. Perhaps
too he is genuinely loyal to his uncle, as he seems to bear him no
malice for breaking his pledged word.

Their love soon reaches such a fervour that Fénice cannot
control herself in public and when she sees Cligés at risk in his duel
with the Duke of Saxony, she cries out in alarm and then faints.
Fortunately for her the crowd misinterpret her actions as simple
concern which she might show for anyone fighting on her behalf,
but Cligés finds them a source of inspiration.

> Clygés, quant Fenice cria,
> L'oï molt bien et antendi;
> Sa voiz force et cuer li randi; (4074-76)

He is not yet aware that she loves him, however, and so when he
seeks permission from her to go to Britain, he phrases his
leave-taking ambiguously as the first hint of his love.

> Mes droiz est qu'a vos congié praigne
> Com a celi cui ge sui toz. (4282-3)

He has sought her permission to depart as courtesy demanded,
and has at least taken his opportunity to speak to Fénice, leaving
her in a state of considerable perplexity. She struggles to reconcile
his apparent declaration of love with his departure from her which
seems to indicate that he does not love her or he would not leave

her to suffer as she does, a suffering which she enjoys.

> Einsi travaille Amors Fenice,
> Mes cist travauz li est delice,
> Qu'ele ne puet estre lassee. (4527-29)

Far more attention is paid to the torments of Fénice, who has after all the more leisure to reflect and so to suffer, for Cligés can find some relief in travel and in action. His love does eventually force him back to Greece, but in great doubt, since he and Fénice are both still uncertain of the other's feelings.

> Mes il n'en est mie certeins,
> N'onques n'en ot plet ne covant,
> Si se demante duremant.
> Et ele ausi se redemante,
> Cui amors ocit et tormante . . . (5040-44)

It is not until some time after his return that Fénice finally creates the opportunity for his declaration of love, by asking him if he had given his love to any lady in Britain. This time Cligés seizes his opportunity and delicately but clearly states his love[11] and is assured that he is loved in return but on conditions.

> Se je vos aim, et vos m'amez,
> Ja n'en seroiz Tristanz clamez,
> Ne je n'an serai ja Yseuz,
> Car puis ne seroit l'amors preuz,
> Qu'il i avroit blasme ne vice.
> Ja de mon cors n'avroiz delice
> Autre que vos or en avez,
> Se apanser ne vos poez
> Comant je poïsse estre anblee
> A vostre oncle et desasanblee,
> Si que ja mes ne me retruisse,
> Ne moi ne vos blasmer ne puisse,
> Ne ja ne s'an sache a cui prandre. (5199-211)

Even at this most intimate and exciting moment Fénice is very much in control of herself and of the situation. Cligés need expect no surrender to passion on her part as she intends to have the best of both worlds — her love and her reputation. Cligés can only suggest an elopement to Britain but he will follow her lead.

> Dites moi la vostre pansee,
> Car je sui prez, que qu'an aveingne,
> Que a vostre consoil me teingne. (5246-48)

His scheme is rejected out of hand as Fénice sees all too clearly that it would produce the very result which she is trying to avoid.

> Et ci, et la, totes et tuit
> Blasmeroient nostre deduit. (5255-56)

Quoting St. Paul in her support that one should avoid criticism,[12] she proposes the scheme of the *Fausse Morte* and orders Cligés to see to the details. With the aid of their marvellous servants Jehanz and Thessala they are able to contrive their escape although Fénice has to endure great torments at the hands of the doctors from Salerno.[13] Cligés really believes that she is dead and is reduced to distraction in the tower until Fénice finally revives, and Thessala is able to cure her from the wounds inflicted by the doctors. Thereafter they enjoy an idyllic relationship, first in the tower and then in the tower and the garden[14] until their discovery by Bertran, who makes no mistake about the nature of their relationship. They are lovers who have lost their secret despite Cligés' violent efforts to preserve it by attempting to kill Bertran. Again their escape is due to the magic powers of Thessala, but with the opportune death of Alis Cligés succeeds to both his throne and his wife. This makes no difference to their relationship, however, as their love only grows stronger and their partnership is symbolised by the fact that they are crowned together. Cligés still looks up to Fénice and continues to treat her as more than a wife, which was only to be expected, as, from the description of the relationship before they were married, there can be little doubt as to which was the stronger character.

> Et s'amie a fame li donent,
> Endeus ansanble les coronent.
> De s'amie a feite sa dame,
> Car il l'apele amie et dame,
> Et por ce ne pert ele mie
> Que il ne l'aint come s'amie,
> Et ele lui tot autresi
> Con l'en doit amer son ami.
> Et chascun jor lor amors crut,
> Onques cil de li ne mescrut,
> Ne querela de nule chose; (6631-41)

The vocabulary is courtly, and so is the idea of the man serving the lady, but the idea of combining this service with marriage is in direct opposition to courtly ideas,[15] and it is clear that for Chrétien this combination represents his preferred solution. The idea is that the lady combines the roles of *amie* and *dame,* attracting in this way the respect due to a wife and the love due to the beloved, and in return the lady loves her husband like her *ami*. Thus passion and duty can be reconciled. The effects are wholly good, as their love increases and is untroubled. A contrast can be drawn with *Erec* 2435 where Chrétien uses 's'amie et sa drue' stressing, according to Luttrell, the immoderate nature of Erec's love. In *Cligés* the legal and emotional ties are, at this point, no longer in conflict as the vocabulary makes clear.

However the poem ends on an ironic note as Chrétien indicates the fate of subsequent empresses, all incarcerated in the gynaeceum, lest they treat their husbands as Fénice did hers. Thanks to Fénice women are worse off than ever, suggesting that Chrétien, typically, has many reservations about Fénice.[16]

In *Cligés* Chrétien is not really concerned with the development of the love between the two couples. Love is love at first sight for Cligés and Fénice and it changes little in intensity thereafter. It is not clear from the text whether Alexander and Soredamors fall in love at first sight, probably not as it is not until the trip to Brittany that love is mentioned, but it is unimportant, as once they realise that they are in love, they too experience the full force of passion. The love of Alexander and Soredamors is straightforward. They are in the story to contrast with the dishonourable behaviour of Tristan's parents Rivalen and Blanchefor, who succumbed to their passion in secret and eventually eloped together. Alexander and Soredamors also contrast with Cligés in that they show how true love between suitable partners in the right context can lead to a happy ending. The sole obstacle to a much more rapid marriage is their own modesty and timidity, which only the intervention of the Queen can overcome. Chrétien devotes much space to analysing the torments of love, the mental anguish and the physical symptoms, which both these lovers suffer, but there is no conflict between them or between them and society. Everything favours their match, and it does indeed turn out to be ideally happy although unfortunately rather short-lived as Alexander soon dies, and Soredamors cannot bear to live without him.

Cligés and Fénice, however, really are in conflict with society,[17] even if Alis is the real villain. They realise that their love is guilty.[18] Cligés is restrained from declaring his love by the fact that it is his uncle's wife whom he loves, while Fénice is so aware of the risk of losing her honour, that she seems to be motivated as much by this concern as by love. Their love is undoubtedly based on physical attraction, and again Chrétien devotes very little space to analysing the nature of the love. Like Alexander and Soredamors Fénice soliloquises on the nature of her love, describes her suffering in which she takes so much pleasure and speculates on how far Cligés returns her love. She seems to be both more introspective and more intellectual than Cligés as he undergoes no comparable self-examination. Instead Chrétien is content to tell us that Cligés suffered, and this suffering is usually translated into action, something which was not, of course, so easy for Fénice. It is indicated that the love between Fénice and Cligés increases, in fact it is stated outright at the end of the poem, but otherwise there is little description of the development of their love. Their first problem is how to declare their love and once this has been surmounted, how to satisfy it. The steadfastness of their love is, perhaps, tested slightly by Cligés' absence in Brtain and then by the suffering undergone by Fénice at the hands of the doctors, but they do not test each other. Once their love has been declared, they have complete confidence in each other, and there is no conflict between them.

Chrétien is really trying to show that *amour-passion* of the type found in the Tristan legend is an uncivilised concept. Certainly no-one can control love in the sense that there is no way of controlling the choice of person with whom you fall in love. Chrétien makes this quite clear in his descriptions of both sets of lovers in *Cligés,* again distancing himself from the control shown in *fin'amors* or *amour courtois.*[19] Once love is recognised, however, behaviour can be controlled. He disapproves of a complete surrender to passion, and none of his characters yield in the way that Tristan and Iseult succumbed to the force of the love potion or indeed in the way that Rivalen and Blancheflor surrendered to their love. Chrétien's characters try to control themselves until they can satisfy their love honourably. This may be at considerable cost to themselves. Alexander and Soredamors both suffer physically because of their love, and at first the Queen puts this down to sea-sickness, although later she realises the truth. Fénice also suffers greatly, and her physical symptoms first alert Thessala. She is adamant that she will not behave like Iseult, as she wishes to preserve her honour. There is no easy solution, however, to this dilemma and the only way out in each of Fénice's successive crises is through the magical powers of Thessala. Chrétien is unable to provide a convincing or realistic solution to the problem and perhaps relies on the parallel with the Tristan legend to make the introduction of magic acceptable. Once the initial use of magic has been accepted there is no reason not to repeat the formula. It may indeed be his intention to show that there is no easy solution to such a situation. Courtly life and great passion cannot be enjoyed simultaneously and passion does involve suffering.[20]

Although the poem is definitely hostile to the idea of *amour-passion* as described in the Tristan legend and strives to show that it is possible to control and direct the emotions so as to preserve one's honour and reputation, it is not a poem which upholds courtly ideals.[21] Courtly influence is undoubtedly there. The language used by the male characters and indeed the whole attitude of the male characters conforms to many of the standards of courtly love. They love from a distance, are prepared to suffer in silence, find inspiration in their ladies, find pleasure in their own pain, accept second place to their ladies and hope to earn their esteem by service and by worth. The ladies, however, are different. Soredamors has no thought of dominance. She accepts Alexander wholeheartedly and without reservation. She does not delay unnecessarily, and neither she nor Alexander seem to contemplate a relationship other than marriage. At any rate when the Queen urges them to get married as that is the most certain way to preserve and increase their love, they are only too happy to do so with all possible speed. Fénice acts otherwise. She does dominate Cligés. She states her terms for accepting his love the moment he has admitted that he loves her. She makes him earn her love by providing the means of escape and throughout their relationship she seems to be the stronger character with Cligés willingly accepting her lead. Their relationship is adulterous[22] which conforms to the courtly idea, and she has an elderly husband who is not exactly a 'jealous' but is undeniably in the wrong. After the initial onset of passion Fénice remains mistress of herself to a remarkable degree, showing great self-control and restraint. She is determined to preserve the secrecy of her affair with Cligés, and the whole affair is conducted with great taste and discretion. Many of these elements are present in the Tristan legend too, but they do illustrate the influence of courtly ideas on Chrétien. The differences emerge at two points: first when Cligés and Fénice admit their love for each other, Fénice will not remain with her husband who is anyway her husband in name only. She is going to avoid adultery as far as possible and will give herself to Cligés only when she is away from her husband. Hence the need for the tower with the secret garden, a sort of other world where the absence of the husband makes the affair seem even more venial than it would at court.[23] Secondly the affair ends in marriage after the convenient death of Alis. Chrétien specifically tells us that after the marriage their love and trust increased and makes it clear that they combined the best elements of an affair and a marriage in their relationship.[24] The determination of Fénice to remain as pure as possible and the happiness of the couple in their marriage are the points where Chrétien breaks away from courtly ideas and stresses his own viewpoint, already forcefully expounded in *Erec et Enide*, that love within marriage is the only way to a truly happy partnership.[25] In *Cligés* both couples illustrate this point, making the contrast with the Tristan legend where neither couple did so.

If it is true that Chrétien wrote *Cligés* as an anti-Tristan,[26] this explains some of his difficulties. He does not satisfactorily resolve the problem of *amour-passion* conflicting with an arranged marriage.[27] He has to resort to magic to resolve the otherwise insoluble. He makes it easier for his heroine to control herself than it was for Iseult in that Fénice is rarely alone with her lover until the story is well advanced. Fénice in particular gives the impression of being extremely calculating. Her very control makes her less sympathetic, although her resolution may be admirable. Then the mechanics of the plot are so important and need so much space that there is less room for characterisation with the result that the characters are less fully developed than in some of the other romances. There is also the point that there is no inner conflict for the characters. They face and surmount external difficulties, but they themselves develop little; and again this is partly because of the mechanics of the plot. As a result this romance is perhaps less satisfying for modern readers than some of Chrétien's other romances. Writing within the bounds of outdoing the Tristan legend seems to have put a constraint on Chrétien, and although the romance is full of good qualities[28] the overall effect is less impressive. It is not a convincing answer to the Tristan legend nor is it a deep study of some aspect of love, for, as has been shown, the love between the couples is barely investigated. His conclusion reinforces the point of view expressed in *Erec et Enide*, but for all the rhetorical brilliance and the learning displayed it remains the less satisfying work, because the psychological insight into the problems of love so vividly displayed in *Erec et Enide* is lacking in *Cligés* and is replaced by intricacies of plot, irony at the expense of the lovers and soliloquies on the effects of love.

Notes

1. Le Gentil, op. cit. 86. 'Dans *Cligés* Chrétien élève une protestation plus directe contre le mythe de Tristan . . . Sans doute Chrétien conte-t-il cette histoire avec une pointe d'humour.'
2. F. E. Guyer, *Romance in the Making* (New York, 1954), 134-40, gives full details on Ovid as a source. P. Haidu, op. cit. 28-30 follows Frappier and Micha in seeing the *Roman d'Eneas* as a source (in addition to Ovid) which already treated the introspective lover ironically. P. Ménard, *Le Rire et le sourire dans le roman courtois en France au moyen âge* (Geneva, 1969), 198, shows that Chrétien describes the love 'avec un discret humour'.
3. P. Imbs, 'Guenièvre et le roman de Cligés', *Travaux de Linguistique et de Littérature,* 8 (1970), 113. 'Alexandre a . . . une conception toute religieuse du culte qu'il doit à sa bien aimée . . .'
4. All quotations are from *Les Romans de Chrétien de Troyes,* II, Cligés, ed. A. Micha, CFMA, 84 (Paris, 1957).
5. K. Uitti, *Story, myth and celebration in old French narrative poetry* (Princeton, 1973), 162, calls this ' . . . romance love — and let us not confuse it with *amour courtois . . .*'
6. P. Imbs, op. cit. 113. 'Soredamors est rebelle à l'amour, et ne veut pas l'avouer, sinon à elle-même, du moins à celui qu'elle aime.'
7. Lot-Borodine, op. cit. 106. 'Encore une fois la prédilection de Chrétien pour le bonheur conjugal se fait sentir dans les propos que tient la reine . . .'
8. Haidu, op. cit. 64-73, argues skilfully that Chrétien's whole portrait of Alexander is ironic showing him to be gauchely uncertain how to behave in a society where a new, courtly etiquette is accepted. 109, he suggests that the elder couple uncertain as to its behaviour in love is contrasted with the younger couple which experiences no such doubts.
9. Ibid. 32. 'Dramatic irony is not only a frequent technique in *Cligés;* it is so basic a strategy of Chrétien's that it largely determines the tone of the romance.'
10. Gallien, op. cit. 64 'Ainsi Fénice et Chrétien ne se bornent pas à condamner l'adultère de *Tristan,* mais aussi toute la conception courtoise où la séparation du cœur et du corps a toujours été de règle.'
11. Ménard, op. cit. 207. 'La déclaration est comique . . .'
12. D. W. Robertson, jnr., 'Chrétien's *Cligés* and the Ovidian Spirit', *Comparative Literature,* 7 (1955), 40, justifiably sees '. . . a certain humour in the disparity between what Fénice is seeking to justify by her authority and what her authority actually says'. Haidu, op. cit. 91-92, sees this note of irony continuing throughout the episode through the 'ironic play between religon and Fénice's actions'.

13. Haidu, op. cit. 98, sees this as ironic, possibly comic, an example of a 'trickster tricked, the comic version of tragic irony'. Thessala's potion prevents her from reacting to the torture of which, however, she is fully conscious.

14. R. W. Hanning, *The Individual in Twelfth Century Romance* (New Haven and London, 1977), 169, points out that the tower represents visually the imprisoning effect of the love affair which, ironically, is supposed to liberate her.

15. R. Guiette, 'Sur quelques vers de *Cligés*', *Romania*, 91 (1970), 77. 'L'aventure de Fénice, prise dans son ensemble, conteste le code courtois.'

16. This irony has been observed by several critics. R. Guiette, op. cit. 83, '. . . Une teinte d'ironie qui est bien dans le caractère de Chrétien . . .' Haidu, op. cit. 57-58, '. . .irony was the basic method of composition in *Cligés*'. M-N. Lefray-Toury, op. cit. 289. 'L'ironie suprême de la conclusion de Chrétien . . .' D. W. Robertson, jnr., op. cit. 41. 'In a sense the whole of the second part of *Cligés* develops towards an ironic conclusion.'

17. Ferrante, op. cit. 144. '. . .*Cligés* where the pursuit of love is actively anti-social.'

18. Pollmann, op. cit. 304. 'Die Liebe is nicht absolut gut, sie trägt die Möglichkeit zum Bösen in sich, aber sie ist auch kein Schicksal sondern willkommene Aufgabe, die Meisterschaft des Willens zu zeigen.'

19. I cannot agree with Gallien, op. cit. 56-57. 'Les idées qu'expose Chrétien sur la façon dont le véritable amour entre dans le cœur sont en parfaite harmonie avec les valeurs fondamentales de l'amour courtois pour qui l'amour comporte une part de raison et une part de volonté.' Soredamors was acting against both her will and her reason when she fell in love. She had after all been 'desdaigneuse . . .d'amors' (440).

20. Haidu, op. cit. 106. 'What does belong to Chrétien is the lesson that this alternative is self-contradictory, that the great passion of the Celtic lovers cannot be accommodated to a more elegant courtly life without incurring the same disadvantages which plagued Tristan and Iseut.'

21. Gallien, op. cit. 68. 'Mais la morale courtoise Chrétien n'en a jamais subi l'influence. . .' He was influenced by it in that he reacted against it. See Ferrante, op. cit. 144 and 150, where she shows how Chrétien uses ridicule to condemn courtly conventions.

22. Fénice's marriage is unconsummated, so that it could be considered to be null and void, but this point is not made by Chrétien. In the eyes of their world, ignorant of the potion, the lovers must be seen to be adulterous. Haidu, op. cit. 106. 'Fenice's love is socially and morally adulterous, whatever the details of the consummation.'

23. Ibid. 103. 'A love lived or endured in isolation is always false for Chrétien.' (cf. Mabonagrain and his lady in *Erec et Enide)* and 'The love of two partners who isolate themselves from the world and other men is, however pleasurable, a living death for Chrétien'.

24. This clearly conflicts with the subsequent ruling of Andreas Capellanus who quotes a judgment of Marie de Champagne to the effect that if a pair of courtly lovers marry, their love must be presumed to be at an end. See Luttrell, op. cit. 58. Guiette, op. cit. 77. 'Toutes les conventions, tous les codes n'avaient peut-être pour Chrétien qu'une importance relative. Parfois, il en sourit de son sourire ironique et narquois.'

25. Lazar, op. cit. 224 sees the originality of Chrétien here but will not admit the break with courtly love. 'En imposant le mariage d'amour comme seule solution possible, Chrétien défend une idéologie de l'amour courtois bien peu commune à son époque. Il est contre la *fin'amors* des troubadours (car elle implique le partage, la vie à trois). Il s'oppose à la passion fatale du *Tristan* (elle aboutit à la mort, en passant par l'adultère). Il intègre les conceptions de l'*amour courtois* dans les frontières d'une vie morale et normale.'

26. Micha, op. cit. xiv. 'Chrétien de Troyes n'est pas, à proprement parler, un romancier à thèse.'

27. Gallien, op. cit. 68. 'Au lieu d'une liberté partielle c'est une liberté complète que le poète réclame pour la femme.' *Liberté complète* is a very sweeping phrase, but Chrétien is certainly supporting a very considerable degree of freedom for the woman (although her successors will suffer for it). Guiette, op.cit. 83, sees his failure to resolve matters as quite deliberate. 'Il se garde de résoudre les problèmes qui en résultent.'

28. Uitti, op.cit. 171. '. . .*Cligés* deserves to be seen as the prototype of a kind of sparkling humorously ironic and delicately contrived fiction so much in favor toward the close of the twelfth century and at the start of the thirteenth.'

YVAIN

Love may not be the main theme of *Yvain*, but it is undoubtedly a powerful force, which motivates much of the action. *Yvain* is to a very considerable extent in harmony with *Cligés* and *Erec et Enide*, as Chrétien is concerned with love within marriage which he presents as the happiest solution. It is not a love without problems, however, and these stem directly from the character' actions. As a result the problems examined are quite different from those of *Erec et Enide*, and *Cligés*, and the relationship of the main characters is also quite different. Chrétien is not repeating himself at all.

Yvain is presented as a brash and reckless young knight, not yet one of the leaders of Arthur's court, and the object of much sarcasm by the sharp-tongued Kay. He is determined to avenge the family honour, marred by the defeat of his cousin Calogrenant at the hands of Esclados le Ros, and impetuously steals away from the court so as to make sure that he reaches the magic fountain before Arthur and his court arrive there. Yvain proves his military worth by defeating Esclados and mercilessly pursuing him into the castle, as Yvain must have proof of his victory or else Kay will not believe him. Yvain has not behaved very well throughout this episode, and once he is trapped in the castle where Esclados is dying, he is made the butt of some ironic humour by Chrétien. He is completely at the mercy of Lunete, who is grateful to him because he alone treated her with courtesy when she once visited Arthur's court. The great hero is helpless and depends on a woman's guile and her magic ring to keep him safe until she can arrange his escape. This note of humour is in keeping with the rest of the early part of the poem, where there is a distinct note of irony in the description of the behaviour of the knights at Arthur's court, quarrelsome and disagreeable, describing their shame rather than their honour, as well as in the description of the Queen, who is as sharptongued as Kay, or in the King who falls asleep at an important festivity. Yvain is not the perfect young knight, then, in the way that Erec seemed to be, although some critics consider Erec unduly cautious; rather Yvain is a knight with a lot to learn.

He first sees Laudine in the course of the search for her husband's killer. Yvain is sitting on a couch, protected by Lunete's ring, while the search rages all around him when Laudine enters the room.

> Vint une des plus beles dames,
> Qu'onques veïst riens terriiene. (1146-47)[1]

She is, however, so frantic with grief that she claws and tears at herself in the traditional way and is ready to commit suicide. Indeed when she sees the blood flow from the wounds of the dead man, regarded as a sure sign that his killer was in the room, she does almost go out of her mind. She addresses a long and bitter speech to the spirit or ghost which she assumes must have done the deed, accusing it of cowardice and treason. Yvain meanwhile has been well and truly beaten by the searchers who have thrashed the couch where he is sitting with clubs, but he dare not move, so that the note of farce is introduced into a scene of high tragedy not only through the treatment of Yvain but perhaps with the exaggerated grief of Laudine.[2] It seems an improbable scene to give birth to love, but Yvain has been overcome by the beauty of the lady, even under such trying circumstances, as his subsequent behaviour makes clear. He is sufficiently in control of himself not to tell Lunete what has happened to him, but asks if there is a place from where he can watch the procession, reckoning that in this way he will be able to see Laudine.

> Mes il n'avoit antancion
> N'au cors n'a la procession;
> Qu'il vossist qu'il fussent tuit ars,
> Si li eüst costé mil mars.
> Mil mars? Voire, par foi, trois mile.
> Mes por la dame de la vile,
> Que il voloit veoir, le dist. (1275-81)

He can barely restrain himself from running out to intervene when Laudine again tears at herself in an agony of grief over the corpse, but fortunately Lunete is still with him to restrain him. Love clearly overrules common sense and self-preservation, and Chrétien is gently mocking the star-struck lover. The contrast is made when he describes Yvain's behaviour as opposed to Lunete's. The opposition between *cortoise* and *folie* suggests that Yvain is being criticised.

> Mes la dameisele li prie
> Et loe et comande et chàstie

Come cortoise et de bon'eire,
Qu'il se gart de folie feire . . . (1305-08)

Her subsequent homily drives the point home. Chrétien is now able to play on the paradox in which Yvain finds himself. Yvain is angry about the burial of Esclados as he has no proof that he has defeated him but family revenge is no longer his sole concern, although he is still smarting at Kay's taunts.

Li radoucist novele Amors,
Qui par sa terre a fet son cors,
S'a tote sa proie acoillie.
Son cuer an mainne s'anemie,
S'aimme la rien qui plus le het. (1357-61)

Yvain is completely in the power of love, presumably overcome by the physical attractions of Laudine.

Qu'Amors s'est tote a lui randue. (1377)

The more he sees Laudine, the more he is attracted by her, although he is filled with despair at the thought that he is never likely to be able to have his wish. The only reason for him to hope is expressed in the cynical comment;

Que fame a plus de mil corages.
Celui corage, qu'ele a ore,
Espoir changera ele ancore . . . (1436-38)

Even Chrétien has to comment on the unusual nature of the situation, indicating his criticism of Yvain's lack of control by the phrase 'an si fole meniere'.

Ne mes ne cuit, qu'il avenist,
Que nus hon, qui prison tenist,
Tel con mes sire Yvains la tient,
Qui de la teste perdre crient,
Amast an si fole meniere,
Dont il ne fera ja proiiere
Ne autre por lui, puet cel estre. (1509-15)

Love and Shame both detain him in the castle, and although he is careful not to be too explicit to Lunete when she returns to talk to him, she has little trouble in guessing what has happened, and decides to help him when the opportunity arises.

Yvain is still a helpless prisoner in the castle with no wish to escape, so much is he under the power of Love. He is again made to look slightly ridiculous by what follows, for while he is dreaming his time away thinking of Laudine, Lunete proceeds to do his wooing for him. The spectacle of the knight, who is in love, helpless, while his fate is decided for him by two women, has a certain irony, at a period when men were expected to do their own wooing, even if it was by submission and service. Lunete's approach is severely practical. She has first to shake Laudine out of her grief for her dead husband and then to concentrate her mind on the possibility of a new husband. She succeeds in reminding Laudine of her feudal duty as ruler of the fountain, which now needs a defender and which they know will soon be attacked by Arthur and his men. As none of Laudine's own knights are capable of defending it, an outsider will have to be imported, and Lunete has already implanted the idea that there are better knights than Esclados was. Challenged to prove this she succeeds in trapping Laudine into the realisation that the man who killed Esclados must be the better knight. Despite Laudine's furious reaction Lunete has managed to awaken Laudine's curiosity and she holds in her own mind the short trial which leads to the acquittal of the victorious knight on the grounds that he had never intended to injure Laudine. Her mind is now concerned solely with this problem, and Chrétien describes her state as follows.

> Et par li meïsme s'alume,
> Aussi con la busche, qui fume,
> Tant que la flame s'i est mise,
> Que nus ne sofle ne atise. (1777-80)

It is going too far to say that she is already in love with Yvain, but there can be no doubt that she is very interested in the idea of a new man, who happens to be Yvain. Her next interview with Lunete proves this, for Laudine adopts a very humble tone towards Lunete, confessing the error of her ways, ready to accept her advice but very concerned about two things; what is the new husband's lineage, and no-one must be able to accuse her of marrying her husband's murderer. Yvain, the son of King Urien is an irreproachable choice as her new husband, and she is so excited at the thought that she cannot wait for his arrival. The grief-stricken widow has changed into the impatient bride. Lunete can distract her only by reminding her that she should hold a council which will certainly advise her to marry again and so free her from any odium. Thus both the lovers are made to look slightly ridiculous, as Laudine's rapid changeability makes her seem typically feminine, according to Lunete, and not to be taken too seriously.

Yvain is made even more of a figure of fun in the scenes that follow, as Lunete amuses herself at his expense by telling him that Laudine has discovered the truth and is furious so that she wishes complete possession of him. Lunete is in fact testing him to see if his love is as great as she has assumed, which he immediately proves it to be.

'Avoir vos viaut an sa prison,
Et s'i viaut si avoir le cors,
Que nes li cuers n'an soit defors.'
'Certes', fet il, 'ce vuel je bien,
Ce ne me grevera ja rien.
An sa prison vuel je bien estre.' (1922-27)

Lunete, Yvain and Chrétien all play on the idea of prison.

Ele a droit, se prison le claimme;
Que bien est an prison, qui aimme. (1941-42)

Once Yvain is actually in the presence of Laudine, he is reduced to a state of tongue-tied terror, and Lunete does not hesitate to bring out the ridiculous side of his behaviour. Scolding him sharply and pointing out that Laudine is not going to bite him she pushes him forward to seek pardon for the death of Esclados. At this he finally finds his tongue and is able to behave like a true lover by offering to accept whatever treatment the lady is prepared to inflict upon him. Laudine quickly finds out that he is in love with her but for Laudine the crucial question is whether he will defend the fountain against all-comers. Once that is settled and Yvain is pledged, there is no more to be said, for Laudine intends to marry him.[3] Her council do exactly what she wants them to and confirm her own choice with pleasure. Thus she is able to reconcile her own wish and her sense of honour.

Tant li prïent, que lor otroie
Ce, qu'ele feïst tote voie;
Qu'Amors a feire li comande
Ce, don los et consoil demande;
Mes a plus grant enor le prant,
Quant ele a le los de sa jant. (2137-42)

Chrétien says that love commands Laudine to act as she does,[4] but in many ways Laudine's approach is purely practical. She is concerned with finding a good knight who must be of high birth to defend her spring. She has a duty to her people as a feudal ruler, as Lunete constantly reminds her, and this seems to be always in her mind. She does not know Yvain except by reputation, but the thought of him is attractive. She likes the idea of finding such a suitable match so quickly, as Lunete has so skilfully roused her curiosity. When she sees Yvain, she cannot fail to be impressed by his physical presence, for Lunete has taken care to make him look his best. She may also find his submissive approach to her taste, since, to a high born lady, who is a ruler in her own right, the prospect of a considerate husband cannot be unpleasant. Yvain's approach is, in fact, extremely courtly,[5] and Laudine is quite prepared to fill the role of the lady, although in public she treats him with great honour, making him stand beside her when he was preparing to sit at her feet. The approach is courtly, and the two participants are able to play the courtly roles, but the intention is not courtly, as Laudine intends marriage, and, as indicated, marriage for very practical reasons. Her position would be fully appreciated by a contemporary audience, who would be unlikely to censure her for remarrying quickly, as they would see the need for a defender for her land.[6] This hard-headed realism on the part of the ladies contrasts with the love of Yvain which they are prepared to use to their advantage, and Chrétien is able to mock his love-struck helplessness revealing a certain irony in his view of the courtly lover, masked perhaps by a veneer of adherence to courtly norms.

The marriage seems to be extremely happy, as Yvain succeeds in replacing the dead man in the hearts of all right from the start. He proves his ability to defend the fountain and at the same time avenges himself by easily defeating Kay, no mean knight, as he has never been beaten before, when Arthur and his court arrive at the fountain. There follows an idyllic week while Arthur and his men relax at Laudine's castle, enjoying the company of the ladies, although Chrétien dryly makes it clear that the flirtations remained within limits.

> Si s'i pooient solacier
> Et d'acoler et de beisier
> Et de parler et de veoir
> Et de delez eles seoir;
> Itant an orent il au mains. (2447-51)

The courtly atmosphere created by these flirtations and by the relationship struck up between Gauvain and Lunete,[7] who becomes his 'dameisele', provides a good introduction for the next episode which represents the first test for Yvain now that he is married. With his marriage he has taken on a new set of responsibilities to his wife and her people symbolised by the need to defend the fountain, but he forgets all this as soon as Gauvain presses him to come away with Arthur's court and leave his wife behind. Gauvain's arguments are specious but plausible.[8] He warns Yvain that if he allows his prowess to deteriorate, he could lose the love of his lady.

> Amander doit de bele dame,
> Qui l'a a amie ou a fame,
> Ne n'est puis droiz, que ele l'aint,
> Que ses pris et ses los remaint. (2489-92)

She would be entitled to look elsewhere, and Yvain must avoid gaining the title of 'jalos'. Instead he must come tourneying with Gauvain and delay the delights of marriage which will then seem all the sweeter. Gauvain admits that he himself would have difficulty in following such advice, which is an implied challenge to Yvain, but it is always easier to give advice than to follow it. Yvain is warned against the fault which Erec committed, but Gauvain's appeal is quite openly that he should leave his new found responsibilities and return to the world of masculine companionship at the tournaments. No thought is given to Laudine or her feelings, and Yvain agrees to seek his 'congé', after some hesitation to judge from the text.

> Mes sire Gauvains tant li dist
> Ceste chose et tant li requist,
> Qu'il creanta, qu'il le diroit
> A sa fame . . . (2539-42)

Clearly it is within Laudine's power to refuse to let him go. Yvain is still behaving like the dutiful courtly lover. He is not exercising the authority of a husband in the way that Erec did without giving it a moment's thought. He phrases his request very carefully as being;

> Por vostre enor et por la moie. (2553)

Laudine, who is in love now as her next speech makes clear, answers as a loving and dutiful wife.

> . . . 'Biaus sire! comander
> Me poez, quanque buen vos iert.' (2556-7)

Although Yvain is ready to accept her authority, she does not exert it. Once she knows his request, however, she states her conditions. Her warning is quite clear as to what will happen, if he fails to keep his word.

> Mes l'amors devandra haïne,
> Que j'ai a vos, seürs soiiez,

> Certes, se vos trespassiiez
> Le terme, que je vos dirai. (2564-67)

This is a measure of the serious nature of her love. She has given herself and her lands to him in circumstances about which she was not entirely happy, as she was anxious to avoid any possibility of blame, and she is now deeply committed to him. If he fails to return, he is not only breaking his word, but he is insulting her and showing how lightly he regards her love. A woman of her rank and character would not suffer such a slight, and her warning must be taken seriously. She grants his pleas for mercy in the case of his illness or imprisonment but she seems to sense what will happen.

> Et neporquant bien vos promet,
> Que, se Des de mort vos deffant,
> Nus essoines ne vos atant
> Tant con vos sovandra de moi. (2596-99)

As a pledge of her love she grants him the ring which will protect any 'Amanz verais et leaus' as long as he remembers his lady. Their leave taking is passionate and tearful, but once away from Laudine, Yvain falls more and more under the influence of Gauvain, and he so much enjoys the tournaments at which he excels and the praise which Gauvain heaps on him that he and Gauvain reach such a point of pride that they set up their own court to which the best knights and even King Arthur come and where Arthur sits among the knights. It is hard not to see this as criticism of Yvain and Arthur.

Yvain is not completely lost, however, because in the midst of all his glory, he suddenly remembers about his wife and that he has broken his word. Only the shame of having to admit this in public makes him restrain his tears. His love is thus by no means dead although he has behaved excessively badly. His inner humiliation will be matched by public disgrace, as Laudine's messenger arrives at court and denounces Yvain in no uncertain terms. This time not even Yvain comes to her assistance on her arrival, showing that standards at Arthur's court are slipping, for when Lunete had come on a previous occasion, Yvain at least had treated her courteously. Now he is denounced as 'desleal, traïtor, mançongier and jeingleor'. He is no better than a thief, and the contrast is drawn between those who truly love like Laudine, who had waited for his return, crossing the days off on her calendar 'an grant porpans' and men like Yvain.

Et cil sont larron ipocrite
Et traïtor, qui metent luite
As cuers anbler, dont aus ne chaut; (2737-39)

Yvain's love at first sight and protestations of love are shown to be fickle and valueless in contrast with the love of Laudine which was based on a more practical approach but was to become deeper and more real. As a symbol of her utter rejection of him Laudine demands back her ring, thus removing her protection and showing him up as a false and perjured lover which he has proved himself to be. When Yvain, overcome by shock and distress, is unable to respond, the ring is torn from his finger, and the messenger departs carefully excluding Yvain from her farewell, just as she had excluded him from her greeting.

The shock for Yvain has been very severe, all the more so as he knows that he has deserved it. His reaction shows that he is acquiring self-knowledge.

Ne het tant rien con lui meïsme. (2790)

Now that he has lost his love, he realises just how much it meant to him.

Mes ainz voldra le san changier,
Que il ne se puisse vangier
De lui, qui joie s'est tolue. (2793-95)

He blames himself; he accepts his guilt and in this context it is not too far fetched to see *joie* as his reason for living. It is no wonder that Yvain suffers a brain storm at this crisis for he is faced with an impossible position. He has suddenly realised the extent of his love and at the same time entirely through his own fault has lost his love with no prospect of recovering it. Madness does, at least, afford him some respite from such thoughts.[9]

Most of the rest of the romance, well over half, is concerned with Yvain's struggle to redeem himself and to achieve self-respect. Ironically the pursuit of worth, which Gauvain had urged upon him, has led directly to the destruction of his worth. As a false and perjured lover he is beneath contempt, and Yvain has lost faith in himself as a knight. On every count, as husband, lover and knight, he is a failure. Chrétien has not spared him, and his madness is a fitting punishment for the frivolous and casual attitude which he has hitherto displayed. His redemption starts with the help of God granted through the hermit, but it takes the magic ointment of Morgue, la sage, to cure him. As a result Yvain is deeply indebted to the Dame de Noroison, to whom Morgue had given the ointment, although he is unaware of the true extent of his debt, and his almost immediate reaction is to see whether he can help his rescuer in any way, in his eyes a purely altruistic offer. Concern for others is a new feature in Yvain's character, and he is soon given the chance to express his gratitude to the lady by defeating her oppressor Count Aliers. He is then in much the same position as he was before his marriage. A rich lady, a ruler in her own right is available for marriage and in fact needs to marry some suitable knight. Yvain is clearly highly suitable. The difference is that, unlike Laudine, the lady is desperately anxious for the marriage or indeed just to become his mistress, and her people are only too willing that her choice should fall on Yvain. The only person resisting the marriage is Yvain, who will not consider it or any other relationship at all. Yvain can clearly resist this sort of temptation without difficulty, and although it is not explicitly stated at this point, it is fair to assume that he can do so because of his love for Laudine and his desire to prove himself worthy of her.

His next step forward is when he chooses to help the lion in its combat with the serpent. Whatever the symbolism attached to these two beasts, Chrétien is quite explicit that Yvain has chosen to support the nobler beast from the best of motives.

> Lors dit, qu'au lion secorra;
> Qu'a venimeus et a felon
> Ne doit an feire se mal non . . .
> Se li lions aprés l'assaut,
> La bataille pas ne li faut.
> Mes que qu'il l'an avaingne aprés
> Eidier li voldra il adés;
> Que pitiez l'an semont et prie,
> Qu'il face secors et aïe
> A la beste jantil et franche. (3356-75)

Yvain, thus, has no thought of reward and indeed expects to be attacked for his pains but is rewarded by the lion's gratitude. How seriously this whole episode is to be taken with the anthropomorphic behaviour of the lion is perhaps open to question, but when Yvain reaches the fountain of Laudine, he is overcome with distress.

> Mil foiz las et dolanz s'apele
> Et chiet pasmez, tant fu dolanz; (3496-7)

Chrétien again lightens the atmosphere with the attempted suicide of the lion,[10] but immediately returns to the anguish experienced by Yvain. He blames himself bitterly, wondering why he does not kill himself, and accepting all the responsibility for his current unhappiness. Beneath the courtly vocabulary as he talks about his *dame* and his *joie*, Yvain's real grief emerges very clearly. He loathes himself for his failure.

Haïr et blasmer et despire
Me doi voir mout et je si faz. (3540-41)

He cannot conceive that anyone can be more miserable than he as his debate with Lunete shows, only to discover that he is responsible for her plight, and that as Gauvain is unable to help, only he can save her from death at the stake. His failure to keep his word did not ruin himself alone, but dragged down Lunete as well, as had been foretold in the messenger's speech (2765-66). Yvain owes his brief happiness in love to Lunete and so is not prepared to let her suffer on his behalf, even although she very generously releases him from any obligation to her. The new Yvain will not shirk any of his responsibilities, as only by meeting every challenge can he hope to regain the esteem of Laudine. Whether he has consciously realised that this is his only course is not yet clear, but certainly from the moment he recovers his sanity he behaves quite consistently, always striving to improve himself as a knight, fulfilling a knight's true duties and not just seeking after glory and adventure as he had done before he became insane.

His next conflict is a very serious one for him, as it is a question of whether he will keep his word. This is the very point on which he has once fallen short and thus caused all his unhappiness, so it is not surprising that Yvain should find this particular problem especially difficult to resolve. He has to choose between saving the beautiful daughter of his host from a particularly unpleasant giant and arriving at the stake in time to defend Lunete. He is in both cases a substitute for Gauvain who is the girl's uncle and Lunete's *ami* (2420), so it is not hard to see in this a criticism of the Arthurian court. Gauvain is away trying to rescue the Queen, and his brother-in-law voices some very sharp criticisms of Arthur for allowing this disastrous state of affairs to come about (3921-34). Yvain, no longer at Arthur's court, is fortunately able to make good the damage caused by the shortcomings of the court. Fortunately for Yvain the giant does arrive in time for the combat to take place, although Chrétien does indicate that Yvain would have kept his word and gone to rescue Lunete if the giant had not appeared.

> Que por po ne li faut par mi
> Li cuers, quant demorer ne puet. (4086-87)

He had, after all, warned his host that he had to be elsewhere by
noon (3943-51). As it is, he arrives just in time to accept the
challenge on Lunete's behalf, but even as he does so his obsession
becomes clear.

> Et lui est mout tart, que il voie
> Des iauz celi, que del cuer voit,
> An quel leu que ele onques soit;
> As iauz la quiert tant qu'il la trueve, . . . (4344-47)

He has, of course, to conceal his true feelings but he cannot take
his eyes off Laudine. After his victory the irony of the whole
situation is brought out by Chrétien as all offer him their service,
not realising that he is already their lord, but even more ironically
Laudine condemns herself out of her own mouth.

> 'Certes', fet ele, 'ce me poise.
> Ne taing mie por tres cortoise
> La dame, qui mal cuer vos porte.
> Ne deüst pas veer sa porte
> A chevalier de vostre pris,
> Se trop n'eüst vers li mespris.' (4593-98)

So Yvain hears from his own lady that she is not behaving well
towards him and that his efforts to regain his reputation are
bearing fruit. He is reckoned to be of considerable worth. His
whole attitude, however, shows that he still accepts that he is
completely in the wrong and can only wait patiently for the
forgiveness of his lady, seconding Laudine's prayer that God may
turn his grief to joy. Yvain's love, it is clear from this scene, is
stronger and deeper than ever. He has learnt much from his
suffering. Laudine, not recognising him,[11] can appreciate his
qualities as the Chevalier au Lion, but as her subsequent
behaviour will show, she is not ready to forgive Yvain who used
her so shamefully.

To help him, Yvain has not only God, should he answer
Laudine's prayer, but also Lunete, who now has more reason than
ever to be grateful to Yvain and promises to do what she can for
him beside her mistress. Once again Yvain will do his wooing by
proxy. The adventures of Pesme Aventure and Noire Espine show
again how easily Yvain can resist sexual and material temptation,
offered in each case and firmly refused. They also mark the
triumph of Yvain over adversaries greater than any he has met

before because the enemy he has to face at Pesme Aventure is 'deus fiz de deable', the very personifications of evil and a more than earthly foe. This adventure which Yvain undertakes altruistically marks the climax of his quest for spiritual redemption. He is now fulfilling his true duty as a knight, ridding society of unwanted evils. Similarly his combat with Gauvain marks his social redemption, as, once his identity is discovered, he is immediately welcomed back into the Arthurian court and hailed as one of the great knights belonging to it. He has measured himself with Gauvain, recognised as the supreme knight of the court, and proved himself to be at least Gauvain's equal. Thanks to Yvain's stalwart defence of the younger sister Arthur's court is given the chance to show itself as the protector of the oppressed, because after the drawn combat, Arthur himself outwits the elder sister and is able to administer a just solution. Nevertheless the impression left by the behaviour of the court is of a place which cannot match Yvain's standards of morality, and it is no surprise that as soon as he has recovered from his wounds, Yvain decides to go in search of Laudine. His love is stronger than ever, and he is so desperate that he cannot live without her love. He will even use force if need be to try to bring about a reconciliation.[12]

> Mes sire Yvains, qui sanz retor
> Avoit son cuer mis an amor,
> Vit bien, que durer ne porroit,
> Mes por amor an fin morroit,
> Se sa dame n'avoit merci
> De lui; qu'il se moroit por li.
> Et pansa, qu'il se partiroit
> Toz seus de cort et si iroit
> A sa fontainne guerroiier, . . .
> Que par force et par estovoir
> Li covandroit feire a lui pes . . . (6511-23)

This is very much a repetition of Yvain's first wooing but the difference is that this time he knows that he is going in search of Laudine and he is a very different man from the impetuous, rash, frivolous knight who went to the fountain to avenge Calogrenant. Lunete again is able to control Laudine and by her advice the Chevalier au Lion is sought, as he alone is likely to aid Laudine, who can assist him in his quest for reconciliation with his lady. Laudine is persuaded to swear an oath to this effect, as Lunete has every intention of restoring Yvain to her. As in the first episode all the decisive steps in the wooing are taken by Lunete. The irony of the whole scene is brought out by Laudine's delight at the successful conclusion of Lunete's search, little realising who the Chevalier au Lion really is. Lunete has trapped Laudine by her oath, and Laudine's first reaction is one of fury. She is a proud woman who has been badly hurt and is still not prepared to forgive.[13]

Her very pride, however, now works against her, because, as Lunete knows, Laudine would not stoop to break her word. The way in which she describes such an act must make Yvain smart.

> Et se ne fust de parjurer
> Trop leide chose et trop vilainne . . . (6768-69)

She accepts therefore that she has to bring about a reconciliation with Yvain. Her words sound discouraging in the extreme, but Yvain evidently sees reason for hope.

> Mes sire Yvains ot et antant,
> Que ses afeires bien li prant,
> Qu'il avra sa pes et s'acorde . . . (6777-79)

He throws himself on her mercy as a penitent sinner. He has paid dearly for his sins, which he attributes to *folie,* suggesting that he failed according to the courtly code as well as a husband. Yvain is on his knees to Laudine, both literally and metaphorically, and she grants him a reconciliation which leads to complete happiness.[14]

> Qu'il est amez et chier tenuz
> De sa dame, et ele de lui. (6804-05)

It is possible to detect a slight softening of attitude in Laudine's final speech, where she agrees to accept his plea to keep him, as he will never fail her again. Otherwise the ending would be too hurried and unrealistic. It is possible to argue, however, that Lunete knows Laudine better than Laudine knows herself and realises that not only will Laudine keep her pledged word, but that she will be secretly not too unwilling to do so.

Much of the romance is concerned with the quest of Yvain for redemption. In effect as the Chevalier au Lion he is the sort of knight that Yvain ought to have been. He protects the poor, the orphans and the wronged and does not indulge in frivolous adventures (such as the adventures which he and Calogrenant had indulged in in the first part of the romance) but makes good the evil effects of the adventures of those like the Roi de l'Isle as Puceles, who is the cause of the adventure of Pesme Aventure. Yvain makes great moral progress, but it is clear from his

behaviour at the fountain when he returns there, from his desire to
see Laudine when he defends Lunete and from his behaviour at
the end of the poem, that throughout he is driven by his love for
Laudine. It was the shock of realising how badly he had betrayed
her which sent him mad, and it is the desire to regain her love
which impels him on his quest to regain his reputation and his self
respect once he has recovered his sanity. Love is crucial to the plot
although there are long passages where it is not mentioned, but its
inspiration must be understood.

Chrétien is breaking new ground in *Yvain*. The romance takes
place against a courtly background, the court of King Arthur,
which at the beginning seems to be held up as an example, but is
subsequently mocked and shown to be very much less than
perfect. By association the standards of behaviour of the court are
mocked, and as long as Yvain is associated with the behaviour of
the court, he is shown to be inspired by less worthy motives. He is
almost a figure of fun in his first wooing, although his love is real
enough. He is prepared to risk his life because of Laudine's
beauty. His approach to marriage is courtly as he is definitely the
suppliant and seems to remain in the inferior position. Laudine
does not overtly exercise her authority, but Yvain certainly accepts
it. He does not yet understand the relationship between husband
and wife, however,[15] and is easily won away from Laudine's love
by Gauvain's arguments about preserving his honour. Yvain is still
very much attached to the standards of Arthur's court, standards
which Chrétien shows to be unsatisfactory as they lead to Yvain's
downfall. The relationship between Yvain and Laudine is not, of
course, strictly courtly, as they are married almost from the start of
it, but within the framework of marriage Yvain is always the
courtly servant of his lady, and Lunete so describes him at the end
of the romance when he is seeking forgiveness.

Dame! pardonez li vostre ire!
Que il n'a dame autre que vos. (6756-57)

The courtly elements in the poem are often mocked either directly
or by making fun of the figure such as Yvain who is following them
at that moment. Yvain often cuts a sorry figure for all that he is the
hero, while Gauvain is shown to act poorly over the affair of Noire
Espine, and the court of Arthur is also held up to ridicule.
Marriage, however, is never mocked. It is treated with great
seriousness as urgent and important business, which once entered
into should be solemnly honoured. Yvain has failed as a knight

and a husband by breaking his word but he never fails in his fidelity which is repeatedly tested by the most charming and desirable of possible brides and *amies*. His love, coupled with the help of the lion, probably symbolising the approval of God, carries him through the most tremendous hardships and dangers successfully. Chrétien is not reworking *Erec et Enide* in *Yvain*. He has certainly returned to the theme of a marriage under stress, and it is undoubtedly possible to draw many parallels between the two romances, and even see the situation in *Yvain* as a sort of mirror image of *Erec et Enide*,[16] but the problem in *Yvain* is quite different. The husband is responsible for the crisis in the marriage. It is his love that has to be tested. His wife has failed him in no way, and so it is not as a couple that they have to prove themselves. Yvain has to learn the difference between the true standards of knighthood, which lead the knight to serve others and thus eventually God,[17] and the false standards of the courtly knight who serves only himself. His love for Laudine is the element which forces him to face this difference and then to strive for the higher ideal, as that is the only way in which he can hope to regain her love. The end result is very similar to that of *Erec et Enide*. The ideal solution is love within marriage,[18] but in *Yvain* the weaker partner is the husband, and it is he who must serve his partner and earn her forgiveness.[19] This can be combined with a superficially courtly attitude but Chrétien's essential message is the hollowness of the standards associated with the courtly code and that true happiness can be found only by those who leave them behind for a higher ideal.

Notes

1. All references are to *Yvain,* ed. T. Reid (Manchester, 1942).
2. Elise Richter, 'Die künstlerische Stoffgestaltung in Christien's *Ivain'*, *Zeitschrift für Romanische Philologie,* 39 (1919), 389. 'Mit grosser, echt französischer Ironie ist Laudine gezeichnet.'
3. A. Diverres, 'Chivalry and *fin'amor* in *Le Chevalier au Lion'* in *Studies Whitehead* (Manchester, 1973), 95. ' . . . Chrétien stresses the feudal relationship between the two at least as much as the courtly and matrimonial links.'
4. Lot-Borodine, op. cit. 215, sees her as shallow but 'sensuelle, sinon passionnée, parce que l'amour de la vie n'est pas mort en elle'. Thus she quickly forgets Esclados although her grief had been genuine. Ménard op. cit. 230, challenges 'shallow'. 'L'auteur d'*Yvain* ne décrit

pas l'irrationnel caprice d'une femme volage, il veut rendre compte d'un bouleversement psychologique.'
5. Diverres, op. cit. 110. ' . . . Yvain behaves strictly in the tradition of the courtly lover . . . his submission is total.'
6. Gallien, op. cit. 42. 'Mais Chrétien ne semble pas désapprouver le remariage de Laudine, c'est là encore un témoignage de son hostilité aux idées courtoises.'
7. Diverres, op. cit. 96. 'This is not *fin'amor* . . . It is mere philandering . . .'
8. Gallais, op. cit. 65, shrewdly analyses Gauvain's reasoning but seems unjust to Laudine. 'Laudine a fait un mariage de raison et Yvain, qui se prétendait "prisonnier d'amour" est bel et bien prisonnier de la Raison d'Etat de sa Dame. Cela Gauvain le comprendra en clin d'œil . . .' Laudine married for reasons of state, but by this point she really loves Yvain.
9. Guyer, op. cit. 210, sees this as an extreme example of the lover's symptoms as described by Ovid.
10. Stevens, op. cit. 74-75. 'We must pass over the extraordinary sophistication of this scene, with its elegant blend of the heroic and the mock-heroic, its core of significance behind the slight, comic grace.' See also Ménard, op. cit. 389-96.
11. M. Accarie, 'La Structure du *Chevalier au Lion*', *Moyen Age*, 84 (1978), 13-34. Accarie argues (25-28) that Laudine has recognised Yvain and sets a trap for him, which he avoids by refusing to tell her his name, saved by 'L'instinct de tous les *fins amans*'. Richter, op. cit. 389, makes the point that Laudine can never really have known Yvain. It is therefore easy to understand her failure to recognise him when he has his visor down, and she is not expecting him.
12. Perhaps this gives the reader warning of 6763. 'Me feras amer maugré mien.' Lot-Borodine, op. cit. 231. 'Voilà donc le plus grand grief de Laudine contre Yvain. Comme on le voit, il s'agit uniquement d'une blessure d'amour-propre, et non de sentiment.'
13. Ibid. op. cit. 232. 'Laudine, orgueilleuse et rancunière, ne peut céder qu'à une force extérieure.'
14. Faith Lyons, 'Sentiment et rhétorique dans l'*Yvain*', *Romania*, 83 (1962), 376. 'Pour expliquer le pardon de Laudine, Chrétien ne met pas en valeur ici les mérites guerriers du chevalier vainqueur. Seul l'attachement à la dame rend possible la réconciliation des amants et le chevalier, en vrai suppliant de l'amour courtois, ne demande rien qu'à titre de grâce.'
15. J-C Payen, 'Les Valeurs humaines chez Chrétien de Troyes' in *Mélanges Lejeune*, II (Gembloux, 1969), 1088. ' . . . Yvain est encore très "adolescent". . .'
16. M. Payen, op. cit. 35. 'La situation est l'inverse de celle d'*Erec*.'
17. J-C Payen, op. cit. 1101. 'Mais . . . surtout dans le *Chevalier au Lion* . . . il dépasse considérablement la doctrine de la *fin'amor*. Il devient peu à peu un romancier de rédemption.'
18. Gallien, op. cit. 47, seems to overvalue Yvain. ' . . . dans *Yvain* il accorde à la femme puissance sur son mari; mais ce n'est là qu'une

phase initiale qui se résout en parfaite égalité entre les époux.' Lazar, op. cit. 247, interprets Chrétien differently. 'Le but de Chrétien consistera donc à montrer, d'abord, que l'amour courtois n'exclut pas la passion, ensuite que certaines exigences de la fin'amors (soumission absolue à la dame, crainte de son autorité . . .) ne sont pas incompatibles avec le mariage.'

19. M. Payen, op. cit. 35. 'Mais ce n'est plus un roman de la *fine amor*.'

LE CHEVALIER DE LA CHARRETE

Le Chevalier de la Charrete differs from all Chrétien's other romances as he deliberately disclaims responsibility for both the *matiere et san*, presumably the plot and the interpretation.[1] This could, of course, be a graceful tribute to the Countess Marie and her patronage but when it is coupled with the fact that Chrétien did not finish the work and handed it over to Godefroiz de Leigni to finish, it must assume greater significance. Certainly Godefroiz seems to have worked with Chrétien's good will;

> car ç'a il fet par le boen gré
> Crestïen, qui le comança: (7106-07)[2]

and may well have been guided by Chrétien in the planning of the last section. It is still strange to say the least that Chrétien should both disclaim responsibility for the inspiration for the romance and fail to finish it. If it is then looked at in relation to the other romances, which he wrote, it can be seen that it is undoubtedly different. In *Erec et Enide, Cligés* and *Yvain* there can be no doubt that Chrétien sees marriage as the ideal state for lovers. In *Cligés* the Queen stresses the advantages of marriage, as the only condition in which love will endure (2266-69). In *Le Chevalier de la Charrete* there is no question of marriage and there cannot be, as the lovers are the Queen, already married to Arthur, and one of the leading knights of Arthur's court. If Chrétien had wanted to extol the virtues of unmarried love before, he had ample opportunity in the affair of Cligés and Fénice, who, however, end respectably married. It seems possible therefore that the theme was not entirely to Chrétien's liking, which would explain his care in making clear the source of the plot and the interpretation and his failure to finish it. The fact that he was working on *Yvain* at much the same time, a romance for which he seems to be entirely responsible and which was more to his taste, would also help to explain his passing the work on to Godefroiz so that he could concentrate on the plot which appealed to him more.

At first sight Chrétien treats the theme of the love of Guinevere and Lancelot with all due seriousness.[3] The poem opens with the abduction of Guinevere and if the Foerster text is followed,

Guinevere first mentions that someone other than her husband is interested in her fate at line 211.

> "Ha! Ha! se vos ce seüssiez
> ja, ce croi, ne l'otroiesiez
> que Kex me menast un seul pas." (211-13)

This does not apply to the Guiot text where the corresponding line reads:

> Ha! rois, se vos ce seüssiez . . . (209)

which cannot apply to Lancelot. The first version makes better sense as there seems to be no reason why Guinevere should whisper such a comment about her husband, but every reason why she should whisper it about Lancelot, although she is careful not to name him.[4] Lancelot himself appears on the scene shortly afterwards when he begs a horse from Gauvain[5] and without waiting to choose the better horse leaps onto the nearer one to save every possible second and rides off to try to rescue his lady. His own horse immediately drops dead from exhaustion, and Gauvain shortly afterwards finds the second horse dead at the scene of a great combat, suggesting that the knight had unsuccessfully attempted a rescue. Immediately after this comes the first test of Lancelot's love. He is on foot when he encounters the cart, which Chrétien is careful to explain brings great shame on any who enter into it. Nevertheless as the dwarf driving it will only consent to give any news of the Queen to anyone who will get into it, Lancelot after a brief inner struggle mounts the cart. Chrétien makes it clear that there is a struggle between common sense and love, which love very rapidly wins.

> mes Reisons, qui d'Amors se part,
> li dit que del monter se gart . . .
> N'est pas el cuer, mes an la boche,
> Reisons qui ce dire li ose:
> mes Amors est el cuer anclose
> qui li comande et semont
> que tost an la charrete mont. (365-74)

Gauvain, who is not in love, considers such an act to be 'molt grant folie' so that the contrast is clearly drawn between the lover, completely in the power of love, and the man who is still in control of his reactions.[6]

The strength of his love is further emphasised when he sees the Queen from the window of the castle where he and Gauvain have spent the night. He follows her with his eyes until she disappears from sight, and when he can no longer see her, he contemplates dashing himself to pieces on the ground below.[7]

> Et quant il ne la pot veoir,
> si se vost jus lessier cheoir
> et trebuchier a val son cors; (565-67)

Only the intervention of Gauvain prevents him from committing the crime of suicide and Gauvain manages to drag him back. He cuts a rather ridiculous figure at this point, emphasised by the acid comments of their hostess who thinks that he has disgraced himself to such an extent that he would be better dead than alive as no happiness can come to him in the future.

The ridiculous aspect of his behaviour is not stressed unduly, and shortly afterwards the lover is contrasted favourably with Gauvain who chooses the easier route to the Land of Gorre leaving the more difficult route to Lancelot, who accepts this uncomplainingly. As soon as he is on his own, Lancelot falls into a deep meditation, his whole mind concentrated on the thought of the Queen.

> et cil de la charrete panse
> con cil qui force ne deffanse
> n'a vers Amors qui le justise;
> et ses pansers est de tel guise
> qui lui meïsmes en oblie,
> ne set s'il est, ou' s'il n'est mie,
> ne ne li manbre de son non,
> ne set s'il est armez ou non,
> ne set ou va, ne set don vient;
> de rien nule ne li sovient
> fors d'une seule, et por celi
> a mis les autres en obli; (711-22)

This long list serves not only to bring out Lancelot's absorption in his amorous thoughts, but also by its over-emphasis to make him seem a little ridiculous.[8] Superficially he is the perfect lover absorbed in the contemplation of his lady, but given the circumstances his lack of commonsense and practicality suggest that Chrétien is viewing him with a certain irony. This is confirmed by the following scene, where Lancelot is quite unaware of the threats of the knight at the ford and remains oblivious of his existence until he is knocked off his horse into the water, cutting a decidedly laughable figure. He has to run after his shield and lance which were floating away and catch his horse before he can joust with his attacker. The moment the action begins, however, any trace of mockery disappears, and he is shown as a formidable warrior. Chrétien allows himself a brief smile at Lancelot's expense, but does not prolong it so as to make it too obvious and offend those who would interpret Lancelot's behaviour as a model for the courtly lover.

Lancelot is promptly subjected to another test by the Hospitable Damsel who demands that he should sleep with her. Very reluctantly he consents, but after the meal is confronted with the attempted rape of his hostess and has to decide whether to rescue her which might jeopardise his search of the Queen. His dilemma becomes comic as he struggles to reach his conclusion.

> honiz sui se je ci remaing. (1105)

He has no choice but to rescue his hostess, which he does only to be faced with the test of his fidelity when he has to get into bed with the maiden. Neither of them undresses completely, and it is clear from the way in which he completely ignores her, that Lancelot is not in the least aroused. Chrétien puts it more poetically, saying that he has no heart, as his own heart is elsewhere.

> Li chevaliers n'a cuer que un
> et cil n'est mie ancor a lui,
> einz est comandez a autrui
> si qu'il nel puet aillors prester. (1228-31)

No woman can distract Lancelot from his thoughts of Guinevere as his behaviour on the ride with his hostess illustrates.

> Cele l'aresne, et il n'a cure
> de quan que ele l'aparole,
> einçois refuse sa parole; (1332-34)

He is only roused from his thoughts when he realises that she is leading him away from the straight path. As he insists on returning to it, he finds the stone by the fountain where lies the beautiful comb. When the damsel finally tells him that the comb is Guinevere's, he almost faints from the sudden attack of passion, so violent that his companion dismounts to come to his aid. This forces his recovery, and so as not to embarrass him the girl pretends to have been rushing to get the comb. She is given the comb but he keeps the strands of hair, belonging to Guinevere, which he worships.

> qu'il les comance a aorer,
> et bien .c^m. foiz les toche

et a ses ialz, et a sa boche,
’et a son front, et a sa face;
n'est joie nule qu'il n'an face; (1462-66)

Again this scene can be interpreted on two levels. Superficially
Lancelot is behaving like a perfect courtly lover, adoring some
token of his mistress in her absence, as it will serve to remind him
of her. Compared with it earthly treasures are valueless. On
another level, however, just as in the scene at the ford, the
exaggerated reaction and behaviour make the reader wonder if
Chrétien is wholly serious in this approach to Lancelot.[9] The
courtly lover is, after all, behaving almost blasphemously in
worshipping other gods and despising the saints. By very slightly
overdrawing the picture so that Lancelot could be accused of
demesure, Chrétien hints that there may be some reservations in
his approach to courtly love, although he is very careful not to let
them emerge too obviously.

The inspiration of love is shown to be very great, for Lancelot is
able to cross the Sword Bridge thanks to the power of love. He is
warned about the perils which he faces, and Chrétien makes it
clear what a formidable obstacle the bridge is. Lancelot is badly
cut in the process, as he has to remove his armour to complete the
crossing successfully. As a true lover he even finds pleasure in his
pain.

A la grant dolor c'on li fist
s'an passe outre et a grant destrece;
mains et genolz et piez se blece,
mes tot le rasoage et sainne
Amors qui le conduist et mainne,
si li estoit a sofrir dolz. (3110-15)

The power of love has carried him across the bridge, but there is
also the virtue in his own character, for King Bademagus has been
watching and knows that only a man free from baseness could do
it.

que ja nus passer n'i osast,
a cui dedanz soi reposast
malvestiez qui fet honte as suens
plus que proesce enor as suens. (3173-76)

To Bademagus' surprise, Lancelot despite his wounds, which the
King thinks need several weeks to heal, proposes to fight
Meleagant just as soon as possible, although to please the King he
agrees to postpone the joust until the next day. Lancelot is

showing all the impatience of the true lover. Because of this very impatience when the battle starts Meleagant gets the upper hand because Lancelot is feeling the effects of his wounds. He does not realise that the Queen and her maidens are watching him, until one of the maidens, guessing the reason why he has undertaken this battle, finds out his name from the Queen and shouts at him to take note of the presence of the Queen, hoping that this will inspire him.

The result is not quite what she intended as Lancelot will not take his eyes off the Queen and so has to fight under an even greater handicap.

> Ne, puis l'ore qu'il s'aparçut
> ne se torna ne ne se mut
> de vers li ses ialz ne sa chiere,
> einz se desfandoit par derriere; (3675-78)

For a few moments the audience are treated to the spectacle of Lancelot waving his sword about behind his back to keep off the attacks of such a skilful and dangerous knight as Meleagant, while keeping his eyes fixed on the Queen. The maiden has to intervene again to put an end to this way of behaving which she describes as 'folemant' and instruct Lancelot on how best to cope with Meleagant. One of the best knights in the world has to be told how to conduct his defence by a girl! Even Lancelot feels ashamed that everyone has seen that he was getting the worst of the fight, but by following the instructions he is able to combine watching Guinevere with the business of defeating Meleagant. Lancelot is inspired by love but, as the girl's comment makes clear, to excess. The sight of the Queen has given him new strength and he is able to control the battle exactly as he wants.

> et force et hardemanz li croist,
> qu'Amors li fet molt grant aïe . . .
> Amors et haïne mortex,
> si granz qu'ainz ne fu encor tex,
> le font si fier et corageus . . .
> devant la reïne sa dame
> qui li a mis el cors la flame . . . (3720-50)

As everyone can see that he is now playing with Meleagant, the King asks Guinevere to intervene, which she is willing to do. Lancelot shows yet another trait of the lover by displaying perfect and instant obedience.

Molt est qui aimme obeïssanz,
et molt fet tost et volentiers,
la ou il est amis antiers,
ce qu'a s'amie doie plaire. (3798-801)

At the risk of his own life Lancelot stops fighting, as he has heard what the Queen wishes, and would not for anything cross her. He is all the more shaken therefore at his reception by the Queen when she refuses to speak to him. Bademagus rebukes her for her behaviour towards the man who has risked his life to save her, but Lancelot humbly accepts his dismissal, although neither he nor Kay can provide any explanation for it, and all are puzzled by the Queen's coldness towards Lancelot. Guinevere's true feelings about Lancelot are only revealed when she hears the rumours of his death. Her immediate reaction is to kill herself, as she blames herself for her harsh treatment of him during his life. She holds herself responsible for his death and regrets bitterly that they have never lain naked together. She quickly decides thereafter that it would be wrong to kill herself as in that way she would be at peace whilst it would be better for her to live on and to mourn for Lancelot, a mourning which she admits she would find sweet.[10]

Mialz voel vivre et sofrir les cos
que morir et estre an repos. (4243-44)

As a result of her grief a rumour of her death reaches Lancelot, who immediately decides to die as in that way he can be united with Guinevere. His attempt is much more serious for he tries to hang himself, but fails, and the whole scene becomes slightly bathetic as those with him do not at first realise what he has tried to do and think that he has only fainted. Ironically he attributes her anger to the fact that he had mounted the cart, which he argues she ought to take as proof of his love and devotion, but the distress of both is soon turned to joy when they hear the truth. Lancelot is made to seem more sympathetic to the reader at this point. For all the farcical element in his botched suicide, his reactions are so spontaneous and whole-hearted that the depth of his love becomes apparent. In Guinevere the initially sincere feeling seems to be replaced by a rather more calculated decision as she finds reasons for staying alive, anticipating even a melancholy pleasure from her decision. She is delighted at the thought that Lancelot would have killed himself for her, although she would have been sorry if it had happened.

Their reconciliation is complete as soon as they set eyes on each
other, for the Queen welcomes him in a way which makes clear
that she has forgiven him. Lancelot then finds the courage to ask
why she had publicly humiliated him and is told that it is because
he had hesitated to get into the cart. He abases himself, admitting
that she is quite justified, although before he had thought that her
anger stemmed from the fact that he had actually got into the cart.
He wishes to talk to her more privately and is told to come at night
to the window where they can talk. For all her sensuous thoughts
when she thought he was dead, Guinevere explicitly excludes
anything other than talking or kissing at the window, not so much
because she is unwilling as because it would be impossible with
Kay lying wounded in the Queen's room. The meeting takes place
but both are frustrated. Their frame of mind is made clear by 'a
desmesure'.

> De ce que ansanble ne vienent
> lor poise molt *a desmesure,*
> qu'il an blasment la ferreüre. (4594-96) (my italics)

Lancelot proposes to remove the bars,[11] and the Queen assents,
prudently withdrawing to her bed so that if Kay should wake, she
will not be involved. Guinevere for all her love has not lost her
sense of caution. Once within Lancelot worships as if at a shrine.

> si l'aore et se li ancline,
> car an nul cors saint ne croit tant. (4652-53)

Chrétien makes a telling comparison between the intensity of their
love, confirming what has already been obvious for some time.

> et s'ele a lui grant amor ot
> et il c. mile tanz a li
> car a toz autres cuers failli
> Amors avers qu'au suen ne fist; (4662-65)

Their love has now become completely physical and sensual, and
yet Lancelot still treats the affair in a near religious way.[12]

> ·Au departir a soploié
> a la chanbre, et fet tot autel
> con s'il fust devant un autel. (4716-18)

Lancelot behaves in a way that is nearly blasphemous, but
Chrétien does not criticise him overtly.[13] There is nothing that is
inconsistent in this scene with the rest of Lancelot's character as
illustrated so far. He is a man of great enthusiasm, completely
under the power of his lady and of his love for her. He has finally
received the greatest reward in her power. It is little wonder that

his reaction should be as exaggerated as his other reactions had been earlier when he found the hairs in her comb or when he heard the rumours of her death. Chrétien presents this reaction very baldly with no comment or expansion of the lines quoted. As a result they stand out amongst the other, more conventional reactions of distress at leaving the beloved, and Chrétien may be indicating his disapproval by allowing them to shock without any comment or explanation.[14]

The result of their affair is that Meleagant suspects the Queen of adultery with Kay[15] and fights Lancelot in a judicial combat to prove this. Naturally he is about to be defeated because he has got the wrong man, when once again the Queen shows her authority over Lancelot when she stops him fighting at Bademagus' request. This is despite Lancelot's oath.

> que se il hui venir me loist
> de Meleagant au desus,
> tant m'aïst Dex et neant plus
> et ces reliques qui sont ci,
> que ja de lui n'avrai merci. (4980-84)

He is as ever completely submissive to the slightest whim of the Queen, whatever the risk may be for himself, as once again Meleagant is not willing to stop fighting and would like to take advantage of Lancelot's defencelessness. After this combat the lovers separate as Lancelot goes in search of Gauvain, who has failed to reach Gorre even by the easier route and illustrates the inadequacies of the man who is not inspired in contrast to Lancelot who is inspired by love.

Again the Queen has to suffer agony when she hears news that Lancelot is missing but this time she has to show joy for the safe arrival of Gauvain while concealing her grief over Lancelot. Only with the arrival of the forged letter announcing his safe arrival at Arthur's court is her joy restored, and she and her companions are ready to leave the land of Gorre to return to the court. There the forgery is discovered, and although the King is distressed about Lancelot, he is so delighted by the return of the Queen that his grief is turned to joy.

> quant la rien a que il plus vialt,
> del remenant petit se dialt. (5357-58)

The lovers do not meet again until the tournament at Noauz which Lancelot is permitted to attend anonymously by the wife of his gaoler, the seneschal. He starts very impressively but as soon as he receives a message from the Queen telling him to do 'au noauz', he becomes the worst knight on the field and is humiliated. The Queen is delighted at this exhibition of her authority and exercises it again on the next day rejoicing over Lancelot's submissive reply.

> . . .'Des qu'ele le comande,
> li respont, la soe merci.' (5856-57)

Now that the Queen is sure,

> que ce est cil cui ele est tote
> et il toz suens sanz nule faille. (5874-75)

she is prepared to allow him to do his best which command he receives with the same courtesy. The Queen rejoices in her possession, overhearing all the marriageable girls longing for this knight in the scarlet armour and knowing that he is not interested in any of them, having just proved yet again, at the expense of his own dignity and reputation, how great his love and devotion are.[16]

There is no further meeting between the lovers in the section written by Chrétien which ends where Lancelot is shut up in the tower.[17] In Godefroiz' continuation Lancelot is involved with Bademagus' daughter, and his behaviour towards her differs greatly from the way he behaved to the unmarried women he met in Chrétien's part of the poem.

> La pucele beise et acole . . . (6678)

He goes on to pledge himself to her.

> Par vos sui de prison estors,
> por ce poez mon cuer, mon cors,
> et mon servise, et mon avoir,
> quant vos pleira, prandre et avoir. (6683-6)

He does not mention love, but he has gone further than ever before to any woman but the Queen. It is possible to interpret this as little more than the conventional service of a knight to a lady who has done him a service, but it seems very fulsome.[18] The point is not developed and when Lancelot reaches the court to take up Meleagant's challenge, the attention shifts back to the Queen. She shares in the general rejoicing at Lancelot's return, but her common sense and discretion are very much in control.

> li rois, li autre, qui la sont,
> qui lor ialz espanduz i ont,
> aparceüssent tost l'afeire,
> s'ainsi, veant toz, volsist feire
> tot si con li cuers le volsist;
> et se reisons ne li tolsist

ce fol panser et cele rage,
si veïssent tot son corage;
lor si fust trop granz la folie.
Por ce reisons anferme et lie
son fol cuer et son fol pansé; (6837-47)

Godefroiz finishes with the lovers on this note, for the rest of the poem is concerned with the defeat and death of Meleagant, but the Queen in this last appearance is fulfilling the role of the courtly lover, determined to preserve secrecy, showing 'mesure' as she controls her emotions, experiencing great *joie* at the sight of her lover (6824) and planning his reward when the time and place are appropriate. There is nothing inconsistent in this presentation of her character with the character which Chrétien developed in the previous 6,000 or so lines. Guinevere is never as unrestrained or as innocent in her love as Lancelot is in his, but she, of course, is in the more dangerous position and has to be careful. She has probably learnt her lesson from the incident of the blood-stained sheets, which she and Lancelot were able to turn to their advantage unlike Tristan and Iseult from whose story the incident is clearly taken. Guinevere presumably had no wish to resemble Iseult in too many other ways.

As can be seen *Le Chevalier de la Charrete* is very different from Chrétien's other romances. It is concerned with an adulterous love affair, in which neither of the lovers considers marriage. Neither lover expresses any remorse for what they do and there is no thought given to the cuckolded husband. Guinevere seems in fact to be the model wife. At the beginning of the poem she is presented as the loyal consort of Arthur ready to humiliate herself to help him, and so it is a considerable surprise to discover that she has a lover, even if only a platonic one at this point. Once she is back at Arthur's court, it is clear from his delight that he has no suspicions about her, while her intention at the end is to ensure that he should have no cause to suspect her infidelity. She exercises throughout the poem written by Chrétien the role of the *dompna*. She is imperious, distant, demanding and socially superior. Lancelot, as her lover, shows his readiness to make any sacrifice for her. He serves her with patience, humility and obedience. He finds his inspiration in her, and life without her cannot be contemplated. When she finally grants him his reward, he treats it as a sort of religious experience and worships the very bed in which they commit adultery. The language is unfailingly courtly, and on one level Chrétien has written a romance which is a description of a highly successful and extremely passionate courtly affair. The relationship between the lovers conforms to the demands of courtly love; the behaviour of the male partner shows the power of love, and even if his behaviour is felt on occasion to be exaggerated, he is after all an idealised lover in a mythical world. He need not conform to reality in every facet.

On another level, however, it can be argued that even within the courtly code Lancelot is not a wholly satisfactory lover. He undoubtedly lacks *mesure*. His uncontrolled reactions at the sight of the Queen or at the discovery of her hair could well betray their love. His attempted suicide at the news of the death of the Queen again shows an uncontrolled reaction. He is even willing to lose his worth for the sake of the Queen, and this was a sacrifice the lover was not normally called upon to make. This also reflects badly on the Queen for the truly courtly lady did not humiliate her lover. Guinevere seems at times to exercise her power for the love of exercising it, so that in a sense she abuses it. Thus she too lacks *mesure*, although she is very much in control of herself in other respects. These points are not stressed by the author, but they are there in the poem and suggest a certain degree of dissatisfaction with the courtly code.

This impression of dissatisfaction is further strengthened by the flashes of humour which keep appearing in Chrétien's part of the poem. It is noticeable that humour is almost entirely lacking from the last section by Godefroiz de Leigni. As already indicated Chrétien more than once seems to mock Lancelot. On several occasions he is made to seem a figure of fun, as when he twice attempts suicide and fails each time. The first occasion, when he tries to throw himself out of the window, is particularly pointed as his hostess draws to the attention of the audience how much better it would be if he actually succeeded. His day-dreaming to such an extent that he is knocked off his horse into a ford and then has to run and retrieve his weapons before he can fight his aggressor is another risible episode. Again his behaviour in his fight with Meleagant is comic, as is the idea that a great knight should need instruction on how to win his fights from one of the Queen's maidens. The humorous scenes are all fairly short, and the humour is not emphasised, as they are usually followed by a more serious episode, showing Lancelot to advantage, which adds variety to the narrative. Nevertheless the humour is there, very similar to the humour in *Yvain,* where the dignity of the hero is punctured, and the ideals of the courtly court of Arthur are shown to be hollow. In *Le Chevalier de la Charrete* the grand passion of Lancelot is shown to have its comic side,[19] and in this way the figure of the hero is cut down to size. He is not superhumanly perfect; rather he has his failings and his weak points, mostly caused by the intensity of his love, which is discreetly criticised through his humour. The love felt by Lancelot not only inspires him and causes him great happiness. It makes him look ridiculous, act like a fool and on occasion lose his reputation.

Guinevere too is not immune from criticism.[20] It has already been suggested that she is not an ideal courtly *dompna* as she abuses her power over Lancelot. She does not show *mesure* in her treatment of him in the same way as she does when considering her own emotions. This abuse of the love which Lancelot feels for her makes her seem an unsympathetic character, and the calculating element in her personality adds to this impression. She finds very good reasons for staying alive after the death of her lover whereas he in the same situation immediately attempts suicide. She is careful to minimise the risk when Lancelot breaks into her room by withdrawing to bed during the crucial few minutes as he rips the bars out of the window. Chrétien himself makes it clear that great as her love is, it cannot match the love felt by Lancelot. Godefroiz confirms this impression of a calculating woman when at the end of the poem he has her carefully deciding to reserve her welcome until she and Lancelot are alone together. Some of this is of course common prudence, but the contrast is made with the generous, unquestioning and uncalculating love of Lancelot, and it is not to Guinevere's advantage. She is well able to manipulate husband and lover simultaneously, and as a result seems to be rather too much in control of the situation to be wholly attractive.

She is, presumably, not at all worried by the considerations that troubled Fénice. As far as one can tell from the poem, she is a wife to Arthur as well as a mistress to Lancelot and so is guilty of exactly the crime denounced by Fénice. Two men share her body, while one has her heart. Whether this is completely true is of course open to question, as Guinevere never indicates that she does not love Arthur, and it is certain that Arthur loves her. Guinevere is in many ways the model wife. She will go on her knees to Kay at Arthur's request to try to maintain the unity of the court. No comment is made on her feelings at the moment of her return to Arthur from the Land of Gorre. Chrétien does perhaps try to lessen the impact of the adultery by placing it in the Land of Gorre, which is even more remote than Arthur's court. Arthur is not present and although it is not quite a case of out of sight, out of mind, he is certainly not considered at all during the episode. The Queen seems to be almost a free woman, and at this point in the poem she is not physically involved with the King. The implication of Godefroiz' remarks, however, is that once both she and Lancelot are back at the court, she has every intention of continuing the affair, which will put her in the position of Iseult with her husband and her lover both possessing her. If Chrétien was sincere, as he seemed to be, in *Cligés,* where such behaviour was denounced and held up for censure, why should he now write about it, apparently complacently in *Le Chevalier de la Charrete*?[21] Part of the answer must be because it was the 'matière et san' given to him by the Countess Marie. Another part of the answer may be that his complaisance was superficial, as he took pains to dissociate himself from the 'matière et san', and failed to complete the poem, which may well indicate reluctance or a loss of interest.

Confirmation of this suggestion, that Chrétien's enthusiasm for the poem was cool,[22] may be found in some of the other elements in the poem. The humour which suggests that he did not take the pretensions of courtly love too seriously has already been mentioned.[23] The possibility that the lovers are not quite such perfect examples of courtly love has also been considered. To all this should be added what can be deduced about Chrétien's attitudes from the other romances which predate or were written at the same time as *Le Chevalier de la Charrete.* From them it can be argued that Chrétien was no friend to courtly love. He abhorred the idea of adultery and preferred to stress the advantages of marriage. Chrétien was also perfectly capable of writing a romance with several layers of meaning.[24] It can be argued that this is particularly true of *Yvain,* which is a straight adventure, a quest for identity, a highly symbolic account of the pursuit of an ideal, a mocking criticism of the claims of Arthur's court to represent *courtoisie* and a love story. The same is surely true of *Le Chevalier de la Charrete.* On one level it is an account of the courtly love affair of Lancelot and Guinevere, which is carried to such a point of idealism that it could only happen in a mythical otherworld such as the Kingdoms of Gorre and Logres. For those who look beneath the courtly surface, however, Chrétien by his use of humour and exaggeration is suggesting that a courtly affair is not the ideal which it seems. The effect of power on the character of the lady is shown to be unpleasing, while the man is reduced to a state of abject submission where his own self-respect and dignity are less important to him than his love. Chrétien is well able to use the elements of a courtly affair but he attempts to turn them against themselves [25] by showing their harmful effects on those involved.[26]

Thus it can be argued that far from writing a poem which extols *amour courtois*, in *Le Chevalier de la Charrete* Chrétien has subtly used the 'matiere et san' imposed on him to illustrate the weaknesses of courtly love.[27] If this theory is accepted, then this romance is not so different from the other romances as it appears at first glance.[28] Although it does not extol the virtues of marriage, it does bring out the drawbacks of the rival code of courtly love.[29] The attitude of quiet criticism expressed through gentle humour[30] and the characterisation of the main characters is very similar to the attitude expressed in *Yvain*. Chrétien's views on love are not greatly altered by the ideas in *Le Chevalier de la Charrete*.

Notes

1. T. P. Cross and W. A. Nitze, *Lancelot and Guinevere* (Chicago, 1930) 68. 'In short, the sens that Mary gave the poet consisted of two main ideas; (1) the extra-conjugal nature of the love affair, symbolized by Lancelot and Guinevere; (2) the deliberate or chosen ob dience of the former to the latter in this relationship.'
2. All quotations are from *Les Romans de Chrétien de Troyes* Le Chevalier de la charrette, ed. M. Roques CFMA, 86 (i a. 1958) except for lines 211-13 which are from Christian von Troyes, *Sämtliche erhaltene werke*, IV ed. W. Foerster (Halle, 1899).
3. J-C Payen, *Les Valeurs humaines* 1093 seems to accept this view. '. . . une sorte d'hymne à une fin'amor exclusive et presque idolâtre.'
   See also Lazar, op. cit. 235. '. . .l'illustration la plus complète et la plus absolue de l'idéologie amoureuse des troubadours.' Z. Zaddy, '*Le Chevalier de la Charrete* and the *De Amore* of Andreas' in *Studies . . . Whitehead* (Manchester, 1973), 366-99, demonstrates how the behaviour of Lancelot and Guinevere conforms to the rules and ideas of Andreas.
4. M. Roques, 'Pour l'interprétation du *Chevalier de la charrete* de Chrétien de Troyes', *CCM*, 1 (1958) 148, is surely wrong to reject any 'délectation spéciale' between Guinevere and Lancelot. See also L. J. Rahilly, 'Mario Roques, avait-il raison?' *Romania*, 99 (1978), 400-404.

5. E. Condren, 'The Paradox of Chrétien's *Lancelot*', *Modern Language Notes*, 85, (1970), 444-45, suggests that, as the horse is a well-known symbol of sexual desire, Lancelot's lack of a horse illustrates his lack of virility. This seems unlikely in view of later developments.

6. D. Shirt, 'Chrétien de Troyes and the Cart' in *Studies . . . Whitehead*, 297. 'In his treatment of the cart episode, therefore, Chrétien reveals his own uneasiness and scepticism about Lancelot's predicament . . .'

7. A. Diverres, 'Some thoughts on the *sens* of *Le Chevalier de la Charrette*' in *Arthurian Romance; seven essays*, ed. D. D. R. Owen (Edinburgh, 1970), 28 argues that Chrétien intends to show that Lancelot's absorption in Guinevere, particularly her physical presence, is excessive; thus he lacks the essential quality of *mesure*.

8. Ferrante, op. cit. 153-54, brings out both the serious treatment of Lancelot's inspiration, love, and the ironic humour.

9. Pollmann, op. cit. 307. 'Wir haben es hier mit einer geschickten Parodie zu tun, die sich ganz folgerichtig in die Gesamtlinie der chrétienischen Romane einfügt.'

10. Lefay-Toury, op. cit. 290. 'Après avoir souhaité périr, Guenièvre se ravise et choisit de vivre mais dans les raisons qu'elle se donne, on sent l'ironie de Chrétien.'

11. Hanning, op. cit. 232, sees this as symbolising self-destruction and social disruption.

12. Pollmann, op. cit. 308. 'Nur im Sinne der Satire kann es verstanden werden, wenn Chrétien de Troyes diese Parallelität gerade in dem Augenblick so ausdrücklich werden lässt, als die Liebe ihrer physischen Erfüllung sich nähert.'

13. J-C. Payen, op. cit. 1098, thinks that this scene would not shock its audience. ' . . . il n'y a là rien de choquant pour une société courtoise qui admet fort bien, dans les conventions d'un amour probablement plus littéraire que vécu, une certaine confusion des valeurs qui provoque plus de sourires indulgents et complices que de gêne ou d'indignation.'

14. Diverres, op. cit. 31-32, suggests that if Chrétien had intended to glorify courtly love, this night would mark the climax of the poem. It does not, indicating his disapproval.

15. Shirt, op. cit. 298, shows how Chrétien here by use of strong vocabulary brings out the true nature of adultery, described in *Cligés* as 'traïson' (6651).

16. Pollman, op. cit. 307. ' . . . hier zeigt Chrétien de Troyes eine in allen seinen Werken gegenwärtige Möglichkeit der Parodie in ihrer Vollendung.' Lot-Borodine, op. cit. 187, sees this scene as a triumph for love. 'En effet, la victoire de l'amour est complète dans la scène du tournoi, la domination de la dame y est asbolue . . .'

17. It is possible that Chrétien saw no solution to the situation. R. H. Thompson, 'The Prison of the Senses', *Forum for Modern Language Studies*, 15 (1979), 252. 'The situation is hopeless. Furthermore this suggests that Chrétien abandoned the poem when he did precisely because there could be no solution to Lancelot's dilemma, further evidence of the poet's basic disapproval of *fin'amor*.' J. F. Benton,

'Clio and Venus' in *The Meaning of Courtly Love*. ed. F.X. Newman,

28. 'Chrétien wrote courteously of Lancelot and left him locked in a tower, rather than condemning him explicitly, not because he found his behaviour admirable but because he was writing in the medieval tradition of irony.'

18. J. Deroy, 'Chrétien de Troyes et Godefroy de Leigni; conspirateurs contre la fin'amor adultère', *Cultura Neolatina*, 38 (1978), 67-78, argues that Lancelot abandons Guinevere for Meleagant's sister because he resented Guinevere making him break his oath to slay Meleagant. At the end of the poem he ignores Guinevere who is building castles in Spain. The verdict on this interesting theory must be not proven. Diverres, op. cit. 35, also wonders if Meleagant's sister has become the *dompna* of Lancelot.

19. Haidu, op. cit. 160, note 119. 'He [Chrétien] enjoyed the humor known as Gallic, especially in the *Lancelot* (perhaps in reaction to an overall assignment he found distasteful).'

20. Lot-Borodine, op. cit. 191, realised this. 'En effet, loin de voir dans Guenièvre l'idéal des perfections de la femme, Chrétien nous la présente au contraire sous des couleurs peu sympathiques.'

21. Frappier, 'Sur un procès . . .', 88, fully realises the anti-social implications of *fine amor*. ' . . . la *fine amor* est dans son principe en conflit avec la morale féodale et chrétienne, puisqu'elle implique une déloyauté envers le mari, qui est aussi le seigneur, puisqu'elle est un amour adultère en pensée et en fait.'

22. I would not agree unreservedly with R. Michener, op. cit. 358. 'It is increasingly apparent that the poet's main concern is no more than pleasing a patroness, a task that seems to disgust him at several points.' Disgust is too strong. Chrétien probably did not care for the subject matter and the interpretation suggested to him, but he was skilful and original enough to use them for his own ends.

23. Ménard, op. cit. 293. 'Chrétien de Troyes laisse transparaître un certain sourire lorsqu'il peint dans la *Charrette* la singulière soumission du parfait amant.'

24. D. D. R. Owen, 'Profanity and its Purpose in Chrétien's *Cligés* and *Lancelot*' in *Arthurian Romance . . .*, 48. 'He [Chrétien] deliberately composed at least the majority of his romances in such a fashion that his public could take them in one of two ways . . . either with straight faces, or with a grain or two of his own mocking humour.'

25. Diverres, op. cit. 24. 'If my reading of the romance is correct, it contains criticism, implicit as well as explicit of both characters' behaviour.'

26. For a completely different interpretation see J. Ribard, *Le Chevalier de la Charrette* (Paris, 1972), who interprets the poem as Christian symbolism.

27. I cannot agree with J. Marx, *Nouvelles recherches sur la littérature arthurienne* (Paris, 1965), 50 ' . . . nous avons montré que la comtesse et le poète étaient bien d'accord pour entreprendre une lourde tâche, la réhabilitation de Guenièvre.'

28. M. Payen, op. cit. 34, sees *Lancelot* as an apologia for *fine amor*. '. . . très opposé à l'idéologie développée dans le *Cligés* et l'*Erec*.'
29. Lefay-Toury, op. cit. 197. 'Quelques indices, quelques scènes, qu'un fil ténu, mais solide, relie tout au long du récit, permettent de le penser et de voir dans *Lancelot*, sans vouloir chercher le paradoxe pour lui-même, non pas un roman courtois, mais son contraire.'
30. Pollmann, op. cit. 308. 'Chrétien de Troyes will eine Liebeskonzeption, die höchste Geistigkeit und ethische Zielsetzung auf ihre Fahnen geschrieben hat, lächelnd parodieren, indem er zeigt, dass das Heiligtum, das der Trobador anbetet, im Grunde doch die Geliebte als körperlich sinnliche Gegenwart ist (cors), die Geliebte als Versprechen der Hingabe.' F. Bogdanow, 'The Love Theme in Chrétien de Troyes' *Chevalier de la Charrette*', *Modern Language Review*, 67 (1972), 50. '. . . a work of pure entertainment' and 53, 'The parody is lighthearted. . .'

LE CONTE DU GRAAL

Le Conte du Graal is the last of Chrétien's romances and is unfinished presumably because Chrétien was unable to finish it through death or ill-health. It is also written for a new patron, Count Philip, whom Chrétien praises at some length in his introduction. This includes a list of Philip's interests and qualities, and an interest in love or romance is not mentioned as one of them. There seems every reason to suppose that the change of patron meant a distinct change of direction for Chrétien's writing. He was no longer writing for a court where sophisticated and intelligent women were important, whose interest in the problems of love and the relationship of men and women is well attested. Count Philip seems to have been an altogether sterner figure, much more interested in religion, and perhaps the more masculine atmosphere of the court would also militate against a great interest being taken in sentimental matters. The introduction not only praises Count Philip for his virtues but stresses the importance of his *carité* suggesting that the tone of the following poem is going to be rather different from the other poems. It also makes clear that the subject was given to Chrétien by the Count himself, who provided the book which is Chrétien's source. This may be nothing more than the usual attempt to bolster the authority of the author by citing an important source, but there seems to be no reason why it should not be true. A new patron with a very different temperament from his predecessor has provided Chrétien with a subject for his next poem, and it is quite natural that it should be very different in character.

It is immediately apparent that the hero Perceval is very different from all the previous heroes of Chrétien. Erec, Yvain, Alexander and Cligés were all young knights or in the case of Alexander on the threshold of knighthood. They were sophisticated young men who were experienced in the behaviour and etiquette of the court and well trained in the arts of fighting. Lancelot was already an established knight and recognised as one of the leaders of the court, a position which all the others would quickly attain. Perceval on the other hand has been brought up by his mother in a remote part of Wales and deliberately kept away from everything associated with knighthood and the court. As a result he is ignorant and naive, appearing almost as a country bumpkin or a Great Fool figure. His ignorance of how to behave is clear not only in his encounters with the knights and in his poor treatment of his mother at his departure, but in his treatment of the *amie* of l'Orgueilleus de la Lande, whom he kisses against her will and whose ring he forcibly removes, acting as he thinks in accordance with his mother's instructions.[1] There is no question of love here on the part of Perceval.[2] Chrétien uses the episode to reveal the naivety, the impatience and in a sense the selfishness of Perceval who ignores the girl's protests that she will be the one to suffer for his behaviour. She is proved correct, for her lover suspects her of infidelity and punishes her severely until sometime later, when Perceval is able to defeat him to prove the innocence of the unfortunate girl. Chrétien is not interested in the love affair of these subordinate characters. The nature of the lover is revealed by his name, Orgueilleus, and his treatment of his *amie* confirms this. Although using courtly terms their relationship does not conform in one important aspect at least, for it is clear that the man is dominant, but Chrétien spends little time on the couple as the main purpose of their existence is to reveal Perceval's way of following his mother's advice with all its unfortunate consequences for others and then later, when they reappear in the story, to give Perceval the opportunity to redeem himself, although the irony of Perceval's behaviour is brought out by the comments of l'Orgueilleus.[3]

Perceval's naivety and ignorance in matters of love are illustrated even more clearly when he reaches the castle of Biaurepaire and meets Blancheflor, its châtelaine. He does not realise that he should take the initiative in opening the conversation, and eventually Blancheflor has to take the initiative herself. Chrétien stresses that Perceval is completely innocent in matters of love.

> Mais il ne savoit nule rien
> D'amor ne de nule autre rien . . . (1941-42)[4]

He falls asleep quite untroubled, and it is only the tears of Blancheflor which wake him as she kneels weeping beside his bed, not daring to go any further than she has already.[5] Finally Perceval takes her into bed, assuring her that it is wide enough for both of them (hardly the attitude of a seducer):

> Lez moi vos traiez en cest lit,
> Qu'il est assez lez a oex nous; (2054-55)

and kisses her. We already know that he knows about kissing as he kissed the *amie* of the Orgueilleus de la Lande and commented on how much nicer she was to kiss than his mother's maids.

> . . . Et il le baisoit
> Et en ses bras le tenoit prise,
> Si l'a soz le covertoir mise
> Tot soavet et tot a aise; (2058-61)

They sleep together but nothing else happens.

> Ensi jurent tote la nuit,
> Li uns lez l'autre, bouche a bouche,
> Juisqu'al main que li jors aproche.
> Tant li fist la nuit de solas
> Que bouche a boche, bras a bras,
> Dormirent tant qu'il ajorna. (2064-69)

Their relationship remains perfectly chaste as is made clear by the use of 'pucele' (2071).[6]

The test of lying chastely together for a night was known in courtly circles but this does not seem to be the explanation here.[7] Perceval is far too ignorant to be testing himself in this way, and Chrétien has already made it clear that he is too innocent to be aware of what is taking place in its full significance (1941-42). This scene is another example of the innocence of Perceval who has no idea of how to behave even after the hurried tuition of Gornemanz. He has acquired enough of the courtly vocabulary to ask Blancheflor for her *druerie* (2104) but the word love is not actually used until the eve of Perceval's battle with Clamadeus.[8]

> Car a chascun mot le basoit
> Si doucement et si soëf
> Que ele li metoit la clef
> D'amors en la serre del cuer. (2634-37)

Blancheflor has been described as his *amie;*

> Li chevaliers, qui se deporte
> A Blancheflor sa bele amie . . . (2416-17)

and her grief and alarm at the prospect of his combat with Clamadeus have been described (2602) so that it is clear that their relationship is developing, with the result that after his victory Perceval is clearly delighted with his situation.

> Et cil qui avoit desraisnie

> Vers lui la terre et la pucele,
> Blancheflor, s'amie la bele,
> Delez li se jue et delite. (2910-13)

His desire to see his mother, however, outweighs all other emotions, overcoming even his initial fear of asking Blancheflor for his *congé* (2922) and despite the grief of Blancheflor which is described in the most perfunctory way (2936) Perceval leaves her abruptly, although promising to return.[9]

Blancheflor seems to represent for Perceval an obstacle as much as the object of his love.[10] He himself does not seem to understand his feelings towards her at all clearly and certainly is not sufficiently skilled in courtly behaviour to respond in the way in which a Gauvain would do automatically. Chrétien does not analyse the feelings of Blancheflor very deeply but it is clear that she falls in love with her rescuer, as is very probable psychologically, and is deeply hurt by his abrupt departure.[11] Perceval is attracted to her and has acquired sufficient polish to observe some of the usages of courtly knights at least in his vocabulary.[12] He is not aware of love, however, and because of the worry in his mind about his mother is to some extent able to resist it, although unconsciously. He has almost no knowledge of the physical side of love and so he and Blancheflor remain virgins,[13] but Chrétien does not seem to attach great importance to virginity. It is not stressed as the supreme virtue as it will be in *La Quête del Graal* where Perceval is and remains a virgin. This whole episode is not important for the analysis of love in it nor indeed for the study of the relationship between the lovers, but for the light it throws on Perceval who is revealed as gauche and immature,[14] although less so than when he arrived at Arthur's court. He has developed into a marvellous warrior able to defeat some of the most famous knights of his time, but emotionally and socially he is still immature, and this is what is stressed so vividly by the description of his stay at the castle of Blancheflor.

The intensity of his feeling for Blancheflor does not emerge until later in the poem at the episode of the drops of blood on the snow. The two colours remind him of the complexion of his *amie*, and he is plunged into a reverie in which he becomes oblivious of his surroundings.

> Si pense tant que il s'oblie. (4202)

Unlike the similar reverie in *Le Chevalier de la Charrete* there is no humour here at the expense of the lover. Chrétien treats the whole episode seriously, and Perceval is not made to look ridiculous. He defeats Sagremors and Kay, but when Gauvain arrives two of the drops have disappeared and the third is fading so that Perceval is less absorbed in his reverie and is prepared to explain his behaviour to Gauvain and to accept his invitation. Gauvain is full of praise for his thoughts.

> Cist pensers n'estoit pas vilains,
> Ainz estoit molt cortois et dols; (4458-59)

Thereafter, however, thoughts of Blancheflor are put aside, for Perceval is back in the world of Arthur and is concerned with avenging himself on Kay. His *amie* is not mentioned again in this scene, and the reader has to deduce the strength of his feeling from the intensity of his reverie and the pleasure which he took in it.[15] How Chrétien intended to develop the relationship between Perceval and Blancheflor cannot be guessed.[16] What is perfectly clear is that he regarded it as very much a secondary theme and indeed that the love relationship between them was of little importance to the story. He does not seem to have been·very interested in Blancheflor either, who like so many second-rank Chrétien characters appears, only to disappear the moment her usefulness has ended. Her relationship with Perceval is viewed almost entirely from the angle of how it affects Perceval's development. He is shown to be naive and untutored in love, although gradually learning something of his own feelings, but at no point does love for Blancheflor seem to be his sole motive. Even his defence of Biaurepaire seems to be undertaken as much from pity as from love in the first instance.

Another aspect of love is revealed through the character of Gauvain. His flirtation with La Pucele as Mances Petites reveals the kindly side of his nature when he takes up the case of a young girl at considerable inconvenience to himself because she hero-worships him. He is naturally pleased and flattered by her admiration, amused as well, but there is no question of love here. This is Gauvain at his most attractive, showing himself to be a truly courtly knight, defending the cause of an unjustly oppressed lady.[17] His flirtation with the sister of Guigambresil's King is another matter. The lady is instructed by her brother's messenger to treat Gauvain honourably.

> Ne nel faites mie a envis,
> Mais trestot ausi de bon cuer
> Com se vos estiiez sa suer
> Et com s'il estoit vostre frere. (5796-99)

This command is received with enthusiasm, and almost as soon as
they are alone together, they talk of love, as anything else would
be a waste of time.

> D'amors parolent ambedui,
> Car s'il d'autre chose parlaissent,
> De grant oiseuse se mellaissent.
> Mesire Gavains le requiert
> D'amors et prie et dist qu'il iert
> Ses chevaliers toute sa vie; (5824-29)

The lady is at least as eager for the affair as Gauvain, and when
very shortly afterwards they are discovered, they are embracing
each other with great enjoyment. The affair does not seem to
proceed any further as Gauvain from then on has to fight for his
life, but the lady, despite the discovery that Gauvain is the enemy
of her people, is wholly committed to him. Gauvain has the
reputation of being a lover of repute, and this is simply another
affair for him. In Chrétien he has relatively few affairs, but his
reputation seems to have been established. Again this episode is
not used for emotional analysis. The couple meet and almost
immediately declare their love. They are proceeding to satisfy it
when they are interrupted. It is not a subtle affair nor one which
shows any observance of the rules normally associated with courtly
behaviour. Gauvain and his lady both behave with refinement, at
least on the surface, but there is no question of restraint or
self-control and as line 5826 shows, Chrétien does not seem to
regard that as a matter for criticism.[18] He accepts that this is a
recognised way of behaving and does not criticise either party. The
lady is called 'cortoise' (5820) while Gauvain still is regarded as the
leading knight of the Arthurian court. In worldly terms he behaves
well.

Chrétien uses this episode for two purposes. The contrast is
made with the unsophisticated behaviour of Perceval, who
behaved so boorishly to Blancheflor. Gauvain shows that he is able
to cope with the most demanding situations. The hollowness and
vanity of the type of behaviour associated with the Arthurian court
are also revealed. Chrétien does not criticise the couple directly,
but it is clear that there is no real feeling behind their relationship.
They are passing the time enjoyably but pointlessly. The outcome
is danger for themselves and distress for all the lady's kindred and
people. The futility and fruitlessness of this sort of affair are made
clear, thus revealing the rather flawed nature of the code followed

by Arthur's court.[20] The episode also serves to complicate still further Gauvain's affairs, which is its prime narrative function. It is obvious that Chrétien is not very interested in the couple or their emotions, as he makes no effort to explain their feelings or elaborate the situation. The couple are introduced, their love is quickly described, and the rest of the episode is concerned with the extrication of Gauvain from the trap. The treatment of this episode confirms that, although Chrétien saw love as an essential part of a romance and would therefore involve his characters in love affairs, he was not in this particular romance interested in the development of love nor in its analysis. Gauvain's next encounter is with l'Orgueilleuse de Logres, a strange relationship in which there is not overt love, but for a while Gauvain meekly accepts the role of her servitor, until Guiromelans informs him that Orgueilleuse is a liar. Her spell is then broken, but while it lasted, Gauvain behaved like a courtly lover, although he himself implied that she was not courtly (7201-06a). Chrétien reveals the uselessness of the love service element of courtly love so that these two episodes in Gauvain's career suggest severe criticism of courtly love.[21]

He does, however, illustrate yet another type of relationship towards the end of the romance when he introduces the affair of Guiromelans and Clarissans. They have never met and have only been able to see each other across the river. Guiromelans is wholly committed to his love, despite the fact that Clarissans is the sister of Gauvain whom he hates. Clarissans seems rather less obsessed with her love and proclaims that she is not yet his 'amie', except in so far as she has promised him her love through messengers.

> Mais il m'a, la soie merchi,
> S'amor donee grant piech'a
> Et si ne vint onques decha,
> Mais si message m'ont proiee
> Tant que je li ai otroiee
> M'amor, n'en mentiroie mie;
> De plus ne sui encor s'amie. (9020-26)

In many respects their relationship conforms to the rules of courtly love.[22] Clarissans is of royal birth and thus socially slightly superior to her lover. He has to love from a distance, to wait patiently and to hope for his reward. She has accepted his love and signalled that she is ready to grant him hers, so that she is not so unfeeling as the courtly lady could be. She does not resemble Guinevere in the

Charrete. Although she has granted him her love, she is not at all pleased to discover that he is claiming that her love for him is so great that it outweighs her affection for her brother Gauvain. This she denies vigorously but the part of the poem attributed to Chrétien comes to an end shortly afterwards before there is any development of Clarissans' reaction to Guiromelans' boasting and before there can be any development in their love through a meeting or a further exchange of messages. Although this episode is interesting as introducing a new sort of love into *Le Conte du Graal,* namely a love which in many respects seems to conform to the rules of courtly love, Chrétien does not have the time to develop the affair. He seems to be more interested in it than in the earlier romantic episodes, as both Guiromelans and Clarissans are allowed to explain their feelings. In this way the nature of their love is analysed, and the possibilities of conflict are made clear. Clarissans may well face a clash of loyalty when her lover and her brother meet in combat and she is not so much in love that she has forgotten her family ties, even although she has never met her brother, as far as she knows. Guiromelans also could well be faced with a dilemma, as Clarissans is not going to react in the way he had so confidently anticipated. These conflicts would give Chrétien ample scope to analyse their love, and the clashes possible between love and family sense of duty on the one hand and love and chivalric honour on the other. Unfortunately there is no way of knowing whether or not Chrétien would have taken advantage of possible clashes for which he seems to be preparing the ground, as his other romances show that he is quite capable of not developing a theme which seems to have been carefully and deliberately introduced. The need to defend the fountain in *Yvain,* for example, is just ignored as soon as it has served its purpose and reintroduced when it is needed again. Similarly in this poem the treatment of Blancheflor has been relatively perfunctory, and although her reappearance would have been possible, Chrétien seems to have directed Perceval's attention towards other, less worldly matters. The Guiromelans-Clarissans episode thus remains tantalisingly incomplete, suggesting the possibility of a return to the sort of analysis at which Chrétien had already shown that he could excel in his earlier romances but offering no certainty.[23]

Le Conte du Graal is clear evidence that Chrétien has changed his subject matter.[24] Love certainly figures in the poem. The hero is shown to fall in love with a particularly lovely damsel in distress, although he does not realise what is happening to him and has no idea of how to behave. His love remains unconsummated and quickly ceases to occupy a very prominent position in his thoughts, one brief episode apart when a chance combination of colours reminds the hero of his beloved's complexion. The nature of the love is barely analysed and the beloved remains a very minor character whose main function is to serve as a further stage in Perceval's development. Love also occurs in the treatment of the second hero Gauvain, where it is shown to be a casual and empty affair between two sophisticated partners or the kindly response of an older man to the hero-worship of a young girl. In neither case is the love element regarded as very important for its own sake. It serves to complicate the affairs of Gauvain, to contrast him with the other hero Perceval, and to add a touch of variety to what could otherwise become a rather monotonous list of combats. There is no overt criticism of Gauvain's behaviour, indeed in the case of La Pucele as Mances Petites there seems to be no criticism at all, but in his other affair the criticism is obvious in the uproar and distress caused by the discovery of his love-making. The only case in which Chrétien seems a little more interested in love for itself is in the last example of Guiromelans and Clarissans, for the love of l'Orgueilleus de la Lande and his lady is used primarily as an excuse to reveal Perceval's naivety and subsequently his prowess and his anxiety to undo the harm he has caused. In Guiromelans Chrétien starts to analyse the feelings of the courtly lover, sighing for his lady from a distance, while Clarissans may well suffer an interesting clash of loyalties, but Chrétien did not finish his treatment of this affair.

The contrast between *Le Conte du Graal* and the other romances could hardly be clearer.[25] Love is rarely introduced for its own sake as a theme worthy of study and analysis. Instead it is there as a necessary part of courtly life, a part which could affect the behaviour of knights, but which is to be accepted as just another element in the factors affecting the characters. The female characters are regarded as of little interest for their own sakes, although Clarissans might have been more fully treated than the others. Love which when misused can have unfortunate consequences is a subsidiary theme. Knowledge of how to behave as a lover is an essential part of the code of a knight, but, as illustrated in the behaviour of Gauvain, it can easily degenerate into what seems to be little more than a sophisticated satisfaction of lust.[26] The contrast with the elaborate analyses of the previous romances is striking, and it seems reasonable to conclude that the change of patron was at least in part responsible. Chrétien himself sketches Philip's character in the introduction and we have little evidence there of an interest in things sentimental. A professional writer like Chrétien was presumably well able to adapt to the wishes of his patron, and the other romances indicate that he was not uninterested in other themes than love. The change of subject may well therefore have represented an interesting challenge to him as well as a practical necessity. At any rate there is no evidence of any reluctance on his part for the change of subject.

Notes

1. Paule Le Rider, *Le Chevalier dans le Conte du Graal* (Paris, 1978), 28-29, brings out very clearly how Perceval overlooks and forgets the conditions and nuances stipulated by his mother.
2. Ibid. 167. '. . . l'épisode de la tente, dans lequel un aspect très simplement alimentaire . . .accompagne ce que l'on pourrait considérer comme la parodie burlesque d'une scène d'amour courtois.' Haidu, op. cit. 132-33, brings out the visual erotic comedy. 'The physical positions are fearfully suggestive.' He adds later 135, '. . . unnecessary for just kissing'.
3. Haidu, op. cit. 185-86, brings out the way in which l'Orgueilleus unwittingly shows up the naivety of Perceval's conduct in both the tent and at Belrepaire, obviously finding it impossible to believe that a man can kiss a woman and not go any further.
4. All quotations are from Chrétien de Troyes, *Le Roman de Perceval*, ed. W. Roach (Geneva, 1959).
5. Chrétien describes her as 'hardie et corageuse' (1955). There is no hint of disapproval of her initiative.
6. cf. *Erec et Enide* 2052-54.
   ençois qu'ele se relevast,
   ot perdu le non de pucele,
   au matin fu dame novele.
   Haidu, op. cit. 159. 'Chrétien has continued the technique of erotic suggestiveness and ambiguity.'
7. Sir John Rhys, *Studies in the Arthurian Legend* (Oxford, 1891) 175, draws a parallel with a Welsh 'bundling couple', suggesting a Welsh source.
8. Lefay-Toury, op. cit. 284. 'Blanchefleur a su parfaitement "faire marcher" Perceval et nous pouvons la nommer malgré son charme "la coquette intéressée".' Haidu, op. cit. 162 calls it ' . . .the manipulations of a young woman as shrewd as she is charming and vibrant'.

9. J. Marx, *La Légende arthurienne et le graal* (Paris, 1952), 211, makes the point that all the hero's love affairs must be fleeting because he is dominated by his Quest. He also attaches importance to the probable fairy origin of Blancheflor. F. Suard, 'Place et signification de l'épisode Blanchefleur dans le *Conte du Graal* de Chrétien de Troyes' in *Mélanges . . . Le Gentil* (Paris, 1973), 804, 'Blanchefleur en effet semble pour l'instant n'être qu'une compagne agréable qu'il quitte sans hésiter . . .'

10. Ménard, op. cit. 269, thinks that Chrétien is deliberately imprecise, '. . . parce qu'il est le premier à goûter le subtil plaisir de l'ambiguïté'. Le Rider, op. cit. 83, has a different interpretation. 'L'amour qu'il a éprouvé pour Blanchefleur lui a fait franchir la dernière étape; il lui a révélé le dévouement gratuit, la prouesse désintéressée.'

11. Haidu, op. cit. 167, note 134, suggests that Chrétien leaves Blancheflor's love uncertain but sees no conflict between love and self-interest (cf. Laudine).

12. A Micha, 'Le *Perceval* de Chrétien de Troyes' in *Lumière du Graal*, ed. R. Nelli (Paris, 1951), 126, sees this episode as 'l'éveil des sens' and 127, Perceval as a 'novice en amour' who will only benefit 'après avoir reçu un suffisant vernis chevaleresque' (129). This love is a necessary first step to a higher love. Lefay-Toury, op. cit. 200, describes Blanchefleur as 'fugitive' but helping 'à affiner la sensibilité du valet . . .'

13. Opinions are divided on this point. W. T. H. Jackson, 'Faith unfaithful: the German reaction to courtly love' in *The Meaning of Courtly Love*, ed. F. X. Newman, 59, 'Perceval may be a boor, crude and unpolished, but innocent he is not . . . There can be little doubt that Perceval enjoyed his night with Blancheflor and that not allegorically.' See Haidu, op. cit. 156-62, for a convincing statement of the opposing case. See also the debate between Sister M. Amelia Klenke, 'The Blancheflor-Perceval Question', *Romance Philology*, 6 (1952-53), 173-78, and Helaine Newstead, 'The Blancheflor-Perceval Question again', *Romance Philology*, 7 (1953-54), 171-75. M. Roques, 'Pour une introduction à l'édition du *Roman de Perceval* de Chrétien de Troyes', *Romania*, 81 (1960), 28, calls it 'une nuit de chaste tendresse'.

14. This is not without its amusing side. Le Rider, op. cit. 127. ' . . . on sourira de la gaucherie du comportement de Perceval avec Blanchefleur.'

15. P. Gallais, 'Le Sang sur la neige', *CCM*, 21 (1978), 37-42, argues that this is a common folklore theme signifying future union and defloration. This is Perceval's dream. J. Grisward, 'Note sur un motif littéraire' in *Etudes . . . Lecoy*, 157, sees this as ' . . .la soudaine révélation de la vie intérieure, de l'amour sous la forme la plus délicatement raffinée, la plus délicieusement courtoise, l'amour de loin . . .'

16. Le Rider, op. cit. 190-92, argues forcefully that ' . . . la rêverie de Perceval se termine sur un adieu à Blanchefleur'. She bases this on the

94

symbolism of the falcon and the successful intervention of Gauvain, representing 'l'amitié virile'. Haidu, op. cit. 189-90, however, sees the unsuccessful, early morning attack of the falcon on the goose as symbolising that Perceval's first meeting with Blanchefleur came too early in his development.

17. Le Rider, op. cit. 251, 'Je ne trouve pas trace dans cet épisode de sensualité ni de donjuanisme. Je n'y vois qu'un traitement tout nouveau du thème traditionnel du chevalier protecteur des faibles et ennemi des guerres de rapine.' She is arguing against the much more critical interpretation of Frappier, *Chrétien de Troyes et le mythe du Graal* (Paris, 1979), 222. 'On sent qu'il est ravi par cette dernière conquête, à la fois menue et délicieuse, ravi au point que ses scrupules d'honneur et de loyauté sont annihilés par le caprice d'une fillette.' Haidu, op. cit. 210-11, feels that Gauvain is made comic by Chrétien parodying the courtly *dame* and her service. The cause is the unelevated one of spiteful sibling rivalry.

18. M. Payen, op. cit. 40. 'Chrétien ne veut pas faire l'apologie de la *fine amour,* mais il s'amuse manifestement à raconter un certain type de comportement amoureux — qu'il ne condamne d'ailleurs pas, au moins explicitement.' Le Rider, op. cit. 240. 'Les chevaliers de Chrétien ne se soucient jamais d'être chastes et participent tous sans aucune gêne à cette "luxure" dont les moines du temps font le péché par excellence de la classe chevaleresque . . . Gauvain . . . se conduit . . . comme un aimable chevalier . . . aussi galant et courtois avec les femmes qu'il est vaillant à la joute.'

19. This does not contradict Le Rider's interpretation, op. cit. 255. 'Gauvain . . . ne cesse pas de se conduire en bon chevalier, aucune de ses actions n'est indigne de lui . . . [Nevertheless] Gauvain n'inspire pas la pitié . . .' because the reader is not involved with him.

20. Haidu, op. cit. 219-20 sees Gawain's adherence to courtly conventions leading him into a position where he is ridiculed and degraded, acting as a doorman, defending himself with a chessboard. Micha, op. cit. 127 sees this whole episode as an example to Perceval. 'Comment on conquiert une belle, comment on la défend contre la canaille déchaînée, l'épisode de la sœur de Guiganbresil nous le dira.'

21. Haidu, op. cit. 238-41 analyses the use of irony by Chrétien to criticise courtly love.

22. It is also a form of *amor de lonh*. Luttrell, op. cit. 155 sees it as a 'skit'. Haidu, op. cit. 243, note 304 sees it as *'amor de lonh* à la Jaufré Rudél' deliberately introduced as Gauvain is too identified with northern French ideas to represent Provençal ones satisfactorily.

23. Another incomplete episode is the Gauvain-l'Orgueilleuse de Nogres one. How would it have developed? M. Payen, op. cit. 40. 'Gauvain est "fasciné" par l'Orgueilleuse de Nogres.' Lot-Borodine, op. cit. 266, sees her as treated with great psychological realism by Chrétien.

24. D. Kelly, 'La forme et le sens de la quête dans l'*Erec et Enide* de Chrétien de Troyes', *Romania,* 92 (1971), 340.

25. Ferrante, op. cit. 159. ' . . . he turns to religion for a set of values that are not bound by worldly conventions.'

26. Jackson, op. cit. 62. ' . . . I have little doubt that [in the *Perceval* Chrétien] intended to make an ironic commentary on the courtly system. He does so in all his works.'

CONCLUSION

Throughout his Arthurian poems Chrétien shows himself to be critical of any form of love that does not find its logical and happy outcome in marriage. He makes it clear by the actions of the characters, by speeches such as that of the Queen in *Cligés*, by the conclusions of three of the five romances, that lovers will find happiness only in marriage. Even in *Le Conte du Graal* where there is no example of married love (and much dispute among the critics as to the probable ending if Chrétien had lived to finish it), no other type of love is shown to be satisfactory.

Chrétien is not such a fool, of course, as to try to pretend that love within marriage will be free from any problems of any sort. This is, in fact, a subject which obviously interests him. In *Erec et Enide* he examines an arranged marriage in which the partners are well matched, so that after the marriage they fall violently in love to the extent that their physical passion becomes all-consuming, and the husband in particular falls far short of the ideal in carrying out the social role required of him as a knight and a prince. The conflict between excessive love and society makes both the husband and wife suffer, because both in different ways are guilty of failing in their duty to society. The husband has relapsed into sloth; the wife has failed to inspire and encourage him to fulfil his duty. They are both immature and not yet fully aware of the importance of their social role as the heir apparent to a kingdom and his future Queen. The situation is made worse by the fact that they are so newly married that they do not yet know each other well. They cannot read each other's minds and when they try to, they are liable to misinterpret what they think they see there. Thus the disapproval of society and a failure to understand and trust each other lead them to mishandle the situation and deepen the rift that arises between them. The adventures which they undergo jointly to re-establish Erec's integrity as a knight cause them both to suffer mentally and physically but as a result they emerge with a deeper understanding of themselves and each other, their trust and confidence in their love renewed, ready and able to resume their place in society and take up the roles for which they are destined. Their own happiness and mutual trust contrast strikingly with the self-centred and sterile love of Mabonagrain and his lady which is rapidly turning sour as Mabonagrain comes to realise the extent to which he is a sacrifice to her conceit, and his lady comes to fear that she is losing him. Their relationship lacks all trust and confidence and causes happiness to none. Yet it is a relationship which conforms to many of the ideas associated with courtly love, but Chrétien shows that it has none of the *joia* which was so important to the troubadours. The atmosphere of fear and suspicion is the natural outcome of a love affair sanctioned by no section of society. Mabonagrain and his lady fled in secret and lived in secret, while Enide, as she points out to her cousin, was married amidst general rejoicing with the blessing of the church and her family.

In his first Arthurian romance Chrétien has the confidence to put forward a viewpoint which was probably not shared by the two circles which were most likely to read his romance. The clerics, who must have taught him and to whose number he may have belonged, saw dangers in too great a love within marriage, which was in any case only second best to a life of chastity and celibacy. The aristocratic circles, where his patrons would be found, were presumably already aware of the southern ideas of *fin'amors*, whose influence was making itself felt in the *Roman de Brut* of Wace some years before Chrétien was writing, where Gauvain is the spokesman for those who believe in the beneficent influence of love. If one accepts the traditional dating for *Erec et Enide* and puts the romance between 1165 and 1170, then Chrétien is reacting very quickly to the spread of anti-matrimonial ideas on love in northern France. Even if the more recently proposed later dating is accepted, towards 1180, Chrétien is still among the first to respond critically in the vernacular to the spread of such ideas.

Cligés approaches love in marriage from a completely different angle. Chrétien obviously has the Tristan legend in mind as the structure of the romance and the references to Tristan and Iseult prove. It is equally clear that he disapproves strongly of the headlong, irresistible passion which sets the lovers against society and leads in the end to their deaths after a lifetime of lying and cheating. Although he is amused by the troubles of Alexander and Soredamors, he uses them to show how love can take its place happily in society when two young people make a suitable match with the approval and blessing of all around them. It is a bonus that they fall in love as soon as they see each other, but neither has any intention of behaving in any way that could be described as dishonourable. In a sense their marriage is an arranged one, as was the marriage of Erec and Enide, because the initiative is taken by the Queen when she realises the nature of their feelings, which neither of the lovers has yet dared to make clear. By way of contrast the affair between Cligés and Fénice is shown to be incompatible with their continued existence in society.[1] They have to lie and cheat; they have to abandon their responsibilities; they have to find their happiness by withdrawing from society and even there their happiness and security are short-lived. Chrétien derives some amusement from showing that even with the help of a sorceress there is no easy way for Fénice to achieve her aim. She has to suffer, and the implication is that her suffering is deserved. The end is bitterly ironic.[2] All that Fénice has undergone, all her planning and lying and suffering, rebound. Her treachery is so well known that, although she herself lives happily married to Cligés, all her successors are strictly confined to a life of seclusion so that they will have no opportunity to behave as she did. Posterity has no respect for Fénice's reputation which she strove so hard to preserve.

Chrétien briefly shows us his preference for love in marriage, a marriage arranged between two suitable partners, but he is mainly interested in other matters in *Cligés*. His hostility to the adulterous passion of the Tristan legend is clear. He abhors the behaviour necessary to satisfy such a passion and deplores its effects on the character of the lovers and the society in which they live. He is not, incidentally, interested in the wronged husband who is largely ignored. What he also shows, however, is that there is no way in which adultery can be easy and painless. Fénice may try to guard her reputation and to achieve her ends through magic with the minimum of suffering but it is impossible. Again she may try to behave in accordance with the conventions of courtly love but Chrétien shows that they too are irreconcilable with society. She can only enjoy her love by isolating herself completely in a magical, fantasy world. The moment the lovers emerge from their isolation, society discovers them, and like Tristan and Iseult they have to flee for their lives. In the end Fénice wins happiness for herself, but other women will pay for it. Chrétien uses a mocking, ironic tone to condemn severely the dishonesty, the violence, in short the evil, which adulterous love introduces into society, whether it be an irresistible passion, such as that experienced by Tristan and Iseult, or a more controlled, calculating love such as that experienced by Fénice and her pliable suitor Cligés. Both types of passion disrupt society and seduce people from their responsibilities. Under a veneer of courtly language and superficially courtly behaviour Chrétien signals his disapproval to the alert reader just as unmistakably as he did in *Erec et Enide*.

In *Le Chevalier au Lion* Chrétien returns to the problem of the clash between married love and social duty. Yvain is very much in love with Laudine but it is an immature, selfish love, as he does not yet understand the responsibilities which he has accepted with his marriage. Again it is a marriage which is publicly approved and is suitable from every point of view, once the slightly inconvenient fact that Yvain killed his wife's first husband has been dismissed. Laudine marries Yvain for much more practical reasons but her understanding of love is deeper and truer than Yvain's. She grants his request for a boon without hesitation and because she accepts that it will be to his honour to leave her, she is prepared to endure their separation uncomplainingly, although her messenger makes it clear just how much Laudine suffered during Yvain's absence. Yvain is seduced by the attractions of a courtly life with its stress on individual honour. He thoroughly enjoys the selfish, irresponsible life with Gauvain, and when he does finally realise what he has done, that in pursuit of one sort of worldly honour he has lost both love and self-respect — his distress is so great that he goes mad. In other words he can no longer live with himself and has to abandon his identity. After he has recovered his sanity thanks to the magic ointment of Morgue la sage Yvain is occupied completely by the quest for a new identity in which he can re-establish his reputation, publicly destroyed at Arthur's court by Laudine's messenger, and, although this is not made explicit by Chrétien for some time, win back the affection of Laudine. Naturally the poet concentrates on the man as he is the sinner, who has betrayed his wife, his love and his duty as both a husband and a lord. Laudine appears only briefly to inspire Yvain anew and unwittingly to condemn her own behaviour. Like Erec and Enide Yvain learns through suffering and endeavour that love has to be earned and that it is not to be regarded as something easily won and lightly cast aside. Even at the end he finds that Laudine has been so deeply wounded in her pride and her love that she is not prepared to welcome him back without resistance. As in his first wooing Yvain requires the help of the intelligent and forceful Lunete to secure his wife, and it was only after re-establishing his worth in his own eyes and those of society that Yvain, realising that life was meaningless without his love, was ready to attempt to regain Laudine.

Chrétien utterly rejects the shallow, courtly ideas of Gauvain which are clearly responsible for the unfaithfulness of Yvain. As I have shown elsewhere, Chrétien consistently mocks the ideas and the characters associated with courtly behaviour. In Gauvain he has the accepted exemplar of courtliness, who is, time after time, found wanting in this romance, so that Yvain has to come to the rescue of those who had expected to be able to call on Gauvain for help. The threat to married love by courtly ideas, even when they do not involve adulterous love as here, is made explicit in the temptation of Yvain by Gauvain, and the need for adherence to a higher, less selfish code of conduct is made clear in the unfolding of Yvain's redemption. Chrétien is upholding marriage as something desirable but difficult in which both partners have their duties and responsibilities, but which, even if as here it begins as partly a marriage of convenience, is the way to achieve true emotional happiness. Thus this romance is very closely related to *Erec et Enide,* both examining the problems of maturity and responsibility in a marriage, the one through the couple, the other through the man who is the transgressor. Both romances point to the same ideal, a happy marriage based on mutual respect with lovers who have tried and tested each other and themselves and who even if found wanting at some point have had the courage and the strength to overcome their weakness, to repent and to achieve a true, mature understanding.

The *Chevalier de la Charrette* is very different, as Chrétien did not choose the subject matter and interpretation for himself, nor did he finish it. Superficially it is a romance which extols a purely courtly affair between Lancelot and Guenevere which culminates in their adultery at the court of Bademagus. On a spiritual level it can be argued that Chrétien is symbolically describing the Harrowing of Hell with Lancelot as a Christ-like figure uniting with the human soul, represented by Guenevere. Chrétien, as has been suggested here and elsewhere, is capable of writing with several layers of meaning, however, and there is certainly a third layer in this romance. There is a vein of irony and mockery throughout, which makes cruel fun of Lancelot and holds up the character of Guenevere to pitiless examination revealing her to be a hard, selfish woman with a coldly calculating streak. She is at least as calculating as Fénice and unlike her seems to have no scruples about following in Iseult's footsteps and sharing her body with two men. (There is nothing in the text to suggest that she does not enjoy sexual relations with Arthur.) The effects on Lancelot of her tyrannous rule are shown to be simultaneously degrading and uplifting. On the one hand he is utterly selfless, careless of his life and reputation; inspired to achieve feats which no other man, not even Gauvain, can achieve. On the other hand he is shown to be a fool, made the laughing stock of society, utterly lacking in control or restraint where his love is involved. The lady is equally lacking in restraint, exercising her power for the joy of exercising it, careless of her lover's life or happiness or reputation. Her intelligence is not impaired, however, as she is careful to avoid any unnecessary risk or sacrifice. She intends to enjoy her love, her status and her husband. Beneath the courtly devotion therefore Chrétien is showing that adulterous love, even when it seems to conform to courtly ideas, can destroy characters as well as inspire them. It is not the ennobling, uplifting love which can benefit others as well as the lovers. Lancelot and Guenevere are selfishly involved with each other and any good that emerges from their relationship is shown to be incidental.

The effect on their own characters, particularly that of Guenevere, is shown to be at best mixed, at worst detrimental. Although this romance does not study the problems of married love, it certainly does criticise adulterous love, even when it seems to comply with the courtly conventions. There is no inconsistency in attitude between this romance and the other romances already studied.

Like the *Chevalier de la Charrette, Le Conte du Graal* stands slightly apart from the other three romances. It is written for a new patron, and love is no longer a major theme. The love episodes are subsidiary to Perceval's religious quest and Gauvain's quest which remains unresolved as the poem is unfinished. Perceval's love affair is chaste and for much of the time forgotten by the hero. When he does think about it again, there is disagreement as to the symbolic meaning of the episode of the drops of blood on the snow which can mean either eventual union or eventual abandonment, depending on the critic. What is perfectly clear is that Perceval is not involved in any sort of adultery and that he knows very little about the nature of love. He is learning but in the process is a source of comedy for Chrétien, and with the poem unfinished all that can be said as regards Perceval is that there is nothing in his behaviour to suggest that Chrétien was in any way varying his view on the desirability of married love.

The role of Gauvain is quite different, although again the interpretation is made more difficult by the fact that the poem is unfinished. Gauvain is involved with three different women and is a witness to the love of his sister Clarissans. His dalliance with La Pucele as Mances petites shows his kindness, perhaps his vanity, but above all the fatal ease with which a courtly knight could be diverted from a major undertaking by the whim of a woman even when he fully comprehends the unwisdom of his conduct. Gauvain does not emerge from this episode too overtly criticised, but he is shown to be susceptible and implicitly the standards of courtly knights are criticised. His affair with the sister of Guigambresil's King is presented without comment as a sophisticated flirtation between two willing partners who are about to satisfy their lust when thèy are interrupted. The distress and trouble which this causes the rest of society are also shown without comment, but the impression is clearly given of frivolous and transient emotions and desires which reflect little credit on either party. Again Gauvain has shown himself only too ready to be deflected from a more important task by the company of a pretty woman. The unfinished episode of l'Orgueilleuse de Nogres also seems to criticise courtly love with Gauvain fascinated by this hate-filled woman, serving her pointlessly as the true courtly lover should. Even the love (based on *amor de lonha*) of Clarissans and Guiromelans has its shortcoming. Chrétien highlights the misunderstanding which can arise between lovers who are separated and in fact have never met. Each of these examples of love is critical in some respect of either the behaviour of the participants or the code of conduct which they are following. Whatever Chrétien may have intended as his conclusion, however he intended to develop the various relationships which had arisen in the course of the poem, it is quite clear that none of them were to be regarded as ideals. They are all seen as either a source of humour or a vehicle for criticism. We cannot be sure that Chrétien would have returned to the ideal of married love in this romance,.as he is clearly occupied also with spiritual love but he is quite certainly criticising casual fornication and many aspects of the behaviour normally associated with courtly love.

Throughout his Arthurian romances then, Chrétien is interested in and concerned with the problems and nature of love. He is generally accepted to be a skilled and penetrating psychologist, well able to portray the pains and pleasures of love, even if drawing freely on his predecessors from Ovid onwards.[3] He is a convinced and consistent critic of the currently fashionable ideas circulating in the circles for which he was writing in that he is opposed to adulterous love and opposed to selfish domination by either partner. He is not opposed, I would suggest, to the refining influence of courtly love on standards of behaviour, but he is opposed to any doctrine which leads the couple to withdraw selfishly from society or to use their love as an excuse for harming society either by direct attack or by shirking their responsibilities.[4] Chrétien is writing for aristocratic circles and he is very much aware that people born to positions of power who have inherited rank and influence have a responsibility to society and eventually to God to use all their gifts constructively.[5] They cannot opt out of life for the sake of love and they should not fritter their time away on frivolous and useless pastimes such as tournaments. In this regard Chrétien is very much in keeping with the church teaching which saw it as the role of the knights to protect the oppressed.

For Chrétien the most advantageous sort of love and the one which is most likely to lead to true happiness is love within marriage. He is not opposed to arranged marriages as they can work extremely well, if those responsible for the arranging take their duties seriously. He is aware that marriage is more than just a contract between two people, particularly in the class for which he was writing, but with care and good-will on both sides arranged marriages or marriages undertaken for extremely practical reasons can work very well, leading to great happiness for both partners. He is utterly opposed to immorality in love, particularly adultery,[6] as then love is selfish and destructive, harming the lovers and the society which surrounds them. True love between suitable partners is an ennobling and an uplifting emotion which can do much good. For all his shrewd understanding of human nature and his appreciation of the practical side of life Chrétien was optimistic in his outlook. His Arthurian romances show that he believed in the good as well as the bad side of love and so, although his romances criticise many of the ideas in circulation in his lifetime, he did not stop at simply criticising or condemning what he did not like.[7] He had an alternative view to offer and it is a mark of his courage and his originality that he should advocate something so unfashionable as love within marriage.[8]

Notes

1. Shirt, op. cit. 290. 'In *Cligés* . . . Chrétien had already made his feelings on adultery known; the deception practised by Fenice . . . is qualified as "traïson" (6651).'
2. Guiette, op. cit. 81. 'Une fois de plus il |Chrétien| s'est livré à un jeu plein d'ironie et de malice.'
3. Pollmann, op. cit. 308. 'In der Tat glaubt Chrétien de Troyes . . . nicht an eine idealistische Konzeption der Liebe, wie sie die Trobadors im "fin'amor" entwickelt hatten. Der Norden ist zu realistisch und zu sehr in christlicher und antiker Tradition verwurzelt, um eine solche dichterische Fiktion aufrecht erhalten zu können.'
4. Gallien, op. cit. 10. ' . . . il assouplira, pourtant, et nuancera à tel point la doctrine courtoise, que l'epithète de courtois ne lui conviendrait qu'en vertu d'une interprétation toute superficielle.' Lefay-Toury, op. cit. 292. 'Nous avons vu que les valeurs courtois n'ont jamais été assimilées par Chrétien.'
5. Frappier, 'Jeunesse de Chrétien de Troyes' in *Amour Courtois et Table Ronde* (Geneva, 1973), 139. 'Il [Chrétien] demande aussi une victoire des amants et des époux . . . sur eux-mêmes. Il est un dépassement personnel à deux.'
6. Foster, op. cit. 19. ' . . . Chrétien "did not like adultery" and tried to reconcile love with wedlock.'
7. Lazar, op. cit. 198. ' . . . il n'était pas tant l'esclave de la mode littéraire. Chrétien était un témoin de son temps, mais aussi un novateur.'
8. Luttrell, op. cit. 56-57, argues that love within marriage was normal in Chrétien's day in romance, following Ovid, but 'Chrétien's day' depends on accepting his dating, and his examples are not numerous from the period well before Chrétien, which means that, if the traditional dating is accepted, Chrétien can be seen as establishing this normality.

BIBLIOGRAPHY

This is a select bibliography containing only the works which are mentioned in the text. There are many other books and articles on Chrétien which I have read and found helpful, but to have included them all would make the bibliography inordinately long.

Abbreviations

BBSIA *Bulletin Bibliographique de la Société Internationale Arthurienne*
       Bibliographical Bulletin of the International Arthurian Society
CCM   *Cahiers de Civilisation Médiévale*
CFMA   Classiques Français du Moyen Age
FMLS   *Forum for Modern Language Studies*
PMLA   *Publications of the Modern Language Association of America*
TLF   Textes Littéraires Français
TLL   *Travaux de Linguistique et de Littérature (Strasbourg)*
ZrP   *Zeitschrift für romanische Philologie*

Editions

Erec et Enide, ed. M. Roques, CFMA, 80 (Paris, 1952).

Cligès, ed. A. Micha, CFMA, 84 (Paris, 1957).

Yvain (Le Chevalier au Lion), The Critical Text of Wendelin Foerster with Introduction, Notes and Glossary by T.B.W. Reid (Manchester, 1942).

Le Chevalier de la charrete, ed. M. Roques, CFMA, 86 (Paris, 1958)

Christian von Troyes, *Sämtliche erhaltene Werke*, IV *Karrenritter und Wilhelmsleben*, ed. W. Foerster, (Halle, 1899).

Le Roman de Perceval ou le Conte du Graal, ed. W. Roach, TLF (Geneva, Lille, 1956. Geneva, Paris, 1959).

Critical Works

M. Accarie, 'La Structure du *Chevalier au Lion*', *Moyen Age* 84 (1978), 13-34.

J. F. Benton, 'Clio and Venus; An Historical View of Medieval Love' in *The Meaning of Courtly Love*, ed. F. X. Newman (see below), 19-42.

J. F. Benton, 'The Court of Champagne as a Literary Center', *Speculum* 36 (1961), 551-91.

R. R. Bezzola, *Le Sens de l'aventure et de l'amour* (Paris, 1947).

R. Boase, *The Origin and Meaning of Courtly Love* (Manchester, 1977).

F. Bogdanow, 'The Love Theme in Chrétien de Troyes' *Chevalier de la Charrette*', *Modern Language Review* 67 (1972), 50-61.

G. J. Brogyanyi, 'Motivation in *Erec et Enide*; an Interpretation of the Romance', *Kentucky Romance Quarterly* 19 (1972), 407-31.

C. Brooke, Introduction in *Medieval Women*, ed. D. Baker, dedicated to Professor R. M. T. Hill, *Studies in Church History*, Subsidia I (Oxford, 1978).

L. Carasso-Bulow, *The Merveilleux in Chrétien de Troyes' Romances* (Geneva, 1976).

M. Coghlan, 'The Flaw in Enide's Character', *Reading Medieval Studies* 5 (1979), 21-37.

E. Condren, 'The Paradox of Chrétien's Lancelot', *Modern Language Notes* 85 (1970), 434-53.

J. Crosland, *Medieval French Literature* (Oxford, 1956).

T. P. Cross and W. A. Nitze, *Lancelot and Guinevere* (Chicago, 1930).

J. Deroy, 'Chrétien de Troyes et Godefroy de Leigni; conspirateurs contre la fin'amor adultère', *Cultura Neolatina* 38 (1978), 67-78.

A. Diverres, 'Chivalry and *fin'amor* in *Le Chevalier au Lion*' in *Studies Frederick Whitehead* (Manchester, 1973), 91-116.

A. Diverres, 'Some thoughts on the *sens* of *Le Chevalier de la Charrette*' in *Arthurian Romance; seven essays*, ed. D. D. R. Owen (see below), 24-36.

H. Dupin, *La Courtoisie au moyen âge* (Paris, 1931).

J. Ferrante and G. Economou, editors, *In Pursuit of Perfection* (Port Washington, 1975).

K. Foster, 'Courtly Love and Christianity', *Aquinas Paper* 39 (London, 1963).

J. Frappier, *Amour courtois et Table Ronde* (Geneva, 1973).

J. Frappier, *Chrétien de Troyes et la mythe du Graal* (Paris, 1979).

J. Frappier, 'Pour le commentaire d'*Erec et Enide*', *Marche Romane* 20, 4 (1970) 15-30.

J. Frappier, 'Sur un procès fait à l'amour courtois , *Romania* 93 (1972), 145-93.

J. Frappier, 'Vues sur les conceptions courtoises dans les littératures d'oc et d'oïl au xiie siècle', *CCM* 2 (1959), 135-56.

P. Gallais, *Genèse du roman occidental; essais sur Tristan et Iseut* (Paris, 1974).

P. Gallais, 'Le Sang sur la neige', *CCM* 21 (1978), 37-42.

S. Gallien, *La Conception sentimentale de Chrétien de Troyes* (Paris, 1975).

F. and J. Gies, *Women in the Middle Ages* (New York, 1978).

P. Grimal, editor, *Histoire mondiale de la femme* (Paris, sans date).

J. Grisward, 'Note sur un motif littéraire', in *Etudes Félix Lecoy* (Paris, 1973), 157-64.

R. Guiette, 'Sur quelques vers de *Cliges*', *Romania* 91 (1970), 75-83.

F. E. Guyer, *Romance in the Making* (New York, 1954).

P. Haidu, *Aesthetic Distance in Chrétien de Troyes; Irony and Comedy in 'Cliges' and 'Perceval'* (Geneva, 1968).

R. W. Hanning, *The Individual in Twelfth Century Romance* (New Haven and London, 1977).

E. Hoepffner, ' "Matière et sens" dans le roman d'*Erec et Enide*', *Archivum Romanicum* 18 (1934), 433-50.

P. Imbs, 'Guenièvre et le roman de *Cligès*', *TLL* 8 (1970), 101-14.

W. T. H. Jackson, 'Faith unfaithful; the German reaction to courtly love', in *The Meaning of Courtly Love* ed. F. X. Newman (see below), 55-76.

W. T. H. Jackson, 'The *De Amore* of Andreas Capellanus and the practice of love at court', *Romanic Review* 49 (1958), 243-51.

D. Kelly, 'La forme et le sens de la quête dans l'*Erec et Enide* de Chrétien de Troyes', *Romania* 92 (1971), 326-58.

H. A. Kelly, *Love and Marriage in the Age of Chaucer* (Ithaca, 1975).

Sister M. A. Klenke, 'The Blancheflor-Perceval Question', *Romance Philology* 6 (1952-53), 173-78.

E. Köhler, *L'Aventure chevaleresque,* translated E. Kaufholz (Paris, 1974).

M. Lazar, *Amour courtois et fin'amors dans la littérature du xiie siècle* (Paris, 1964).

M-N Lefay-Toury, 'Roman breton et mythes courtois; l'évolution du personnage féminin dans les romans de Chrétien de Troyes', *CCM* 15 (1972) 193-204 and 283-93.

Y. Lefevre in *Histoire mondiale de la femme,* Volume II, ed. P. Grimal (Paris).

P. Le Gentil, *La Littérature française du moyen âge* (Paris, 1968).

J. Le Goff, *La Civilisation de l'occident médiéval* (Paris, 1972).

P. Le Rider, *Le Chevalier dans le Conte du Graal de Chrétien de Troyes* (Paris, 1978).

M. Lot-Borodine, *La Femme et l'amour au xiie siècle d'après les poèmes de Chrétien de Troyes* (Paris, 1909).

C. Luttrell, *The Creation of the first Arthurian Romance: A Quest* (London, 1974).

F. Lyons, 'Sentiment et rhétorique dans l'*Yvain',* *Romania* 83 (1962), 370-77.

Marguerite de Navarre, *L'Heptaméron,* ed. M. François (Paris, 1960).

J. Marx, *La Légende arthurienne et la graal* (Paris, 1952).

J. Marx, *Nouvelles recherches sur la litterature arthurienne* (Paris, 1965).

P. Ménard, *Le Rire et le sourire dans le roman courtois en France au moyen âge (1150-1250)* (Geneva, 1969).

A. Micha, 'Le *Perceval* de Chrétien de Troyes: roman éducatif' in *Lumière du Graal,* ed. R. Nelli (Paris, 1951).

R. Michener, 'Courtly Love in Chrétien de Troyes: the "demande d'amour" ', *Studia Neophilologica* 42 (1970), 353-60.

J. Moore, 'Love in Twelfth Century France', *Traditio* 24 (1968), 429-42.

F. X. Newman, editor *The Meaning of Courtly Love* (Albany, N.Y., 1968).

H. Newstead, 'The Blancheflor-Perceval Question again', *Romance Philology* 7 (1953-54), 171-75.

P. S. Noble, 'The Character of Guinevere in the Arthurian Romances of Chrétien de Troyes', *Modern Language Review* 67 (1972), 524-35.

P. S. Noble, 'Kay the Seneschal in Chrétien de Troyes and his Predecessors', *Reading Medieval Studies* 1 (1975), 55-70.

D. D. R. Owen, editor, *Arthurian Romance: Seven Essays* (Edinburgh, London, 1970).

D. D. R. Owen, 'Profanity and its purpose in Chrétien's *Cligés* and *Lancelot'* in above, 37-48.

J-C Payen, *Le Motif du repentir dans la littérature française médiévale (des origines à 1230)* (Geneva, 1968).

J-C Payen, 'Les Valeurs humaines chez Chrétien de Troyes' in *Mélanges Rita Lejeune* (Gembloux, 1969), 1087-1101.

M. Payen, *Les Origines de la courtoisie dans la littérature française médiévale* (Paris, 1966-67).

L. Pollman, *Die Liebe in der hochmittelalterlichen Literatur Frankreichs* (Frankfurt, 1966).

A. Press, 'Le Comportement d'Erec envers Enide dans le roman de Chrétien de Troyes', *Romania* 90 (1969), 529-38.

L. J. Rahilly, 'Mario Roques, avait-il raison?', *Romania* 99 (1978), 400-4.

Sir John Rhys, *Studies in the Arthurian Legend* (Oxford, 1891).

J. Ribard, *Le Chevalier de la Charrette* (Paris, 1972).

E. Richter, 'Die künstlerische Stoffgestaltung in Christien's *Ivain*', *ZrP* 39 (1919), 385-97.

D. W. Robertson, jnr., 'Chrétien's *Cligés* and the Ovidian Spirit', *Comparative Literature* 7 (1955), 32-42.

D. W. Robertson, jnr., 'The Concept of Courtly Love as an Impediment to the Understanding of Medieval Texts' in *The Meaning of Courtly Love*, ed. F. X. Newman, 1-18. (see Newman).

D. W. Robertson, jnr., 'The Subject of the *De Amore* of Andreas Capellanus', *Modern Philology* 50 (1952-53), 145-61.

M. Roques, 'Pour l'interprétation du *Chevalier de la charrete* de Chrétien de Troyes', *CCM* 1 (1958), 141-52.

M. Roques, 'Pour une introduction à l'édition du *Roman de Perceval* de Chrétien de Troyes', *Romania* 81 (1960), 1-36.

B. N. Sargent-Baur, 'Erec's Enide; "sa fame ou s'amie"?', *Romance Philology*, 33 (1980), 373-87.

B. N. Sargent, 'A Medieval Commentary on Andreas Capellanus', *Romania* 94 (1973), 528-41.

E. S. Sheldon, 'Why does Chrétien's Erec treat Enide so harshly?', *Romanic Review* 5 (1914), 115-26.

D. J. Shirt, 'Chrétien de Troyes and the Cart' in *Studies Frederick Whitehead* (Manchester, 1973), 279-301.

J. Stevens, *Medieval Romance: Themes and Approaches* (London, 1973).

F. Suard, 'Place et signification de l'épisode Blanchefleur dans le *Conte du Graal* de Chrétien de Troyes' in *Mélanges Pierre Le Gentil* (Paris, 1973), 803-10.

M. Thiebaux, *The Stag of Love* (Ithaca and London, 1974).

R. H. Thompson, 'The Prison of the Senses', *FMLS* 15 (1979), 249-54.

K. Uitti, *Story, myth and celebration in old French narrative poetry 1050-1200* (Princeton, 1973).

F. L. Utley 'Must we abandon the concept of courtly love?', *Medievalia et Humanistica*, New Series, 3 (1972), 299-322.

B. Wind, 'Ce jeu subtil, l'amour courtois' in *Mélanges Rita Lejeune* (Gembloux, 1969), 1257-61.

Z. P. Zaddy, '*Le Chevalier de la charrete* and the *De Amore* of Andreas' in *Studies Frederick Whitehead* (Manchester, 1973), 363-99.

Z. P. Zaddy, 'Pourquoi Erec se décide-t-il à partir en voyage avec Enide?', *CCM* 7 (1964), 179-85.

M-C Zai, *Les Chansons courtoises de Chrétien de Troyes* (Berne and Frankfurt, 1974).